Guide to Teaching 14–19

Other titles in the Essential FE Toolkit Series

Books for lecturers

Teaching Adults – Amanda Hayes

Teaching the FE Curriculum – Mark Weyers

e-Learning in FE – John Whalley, Theresa Welch and Lee Williamson

FE Lecturer's Survival Guide – Angela Steward

FE Lecturer's Guide to Diversity and Inclusion – Anne-Marie Wright, Sue Colquhoun, Jane Speare and Tracey Partridge.

How to Manage Stress in FE – Elizabeth Hartney

Ultimate FE Lecturer's Handbook – Ros Clow and Trevor Dawn

A to Z of Teaching in FE – Angela Steward

Getting the Buggers Motivated in FE – Susan Wallace

How to Teach in FE with a Hangover – Angela Steward

Books for managers

Everything You Need to Know about FE Policy – Yvonne Hillier

Middle Management in FE – Ann Briggs

Managing Higher Education in Colleges – Gareth Parry, Anne Thompson and Penny Blackie

Survival Guide for College Managers and Leaders – David Collins

Guide to Leadership and Governance in FE – Adrian Perry

Guide to Financial Management in FE – Julian Gravatt

Guide to Race Equality in FE – Beulah Ainley

Ultimate FE Leadership and Management Handbook – Jill Jameson and Ian McNay

A to Z for Every Manager in FE – Susan Wallace and Jonathan Gravells

Guide to VET – Christopher Winch and Terry Hyland

Guide to Teaching 14–19

James Ogunleye

continuum
LONDON • NEW YORK

Continuum International Publishing Group
The Tower Building
11 York Road
London SE1 7NX

80 Maiden Lane, Suite 704
New York
NY 10038

www.continuumbooks.com

British Library Cataloguing-in-Publication Data
A catalogue record for this book is available from the British Library.

ISBN: 0 8264 8719 X (paperback)
      978 0 8264 8719 3 (paperback)

Library of Congress Cataloging-in-Publication Data
A catalog record for this book is available from the Library of Congress.

Typeset by RefineCatch Limited, Bungay, Suffolk
Printed and bound in Great Britain by
Ashford Colour Press, Gosport, Hampshire

Contents

Series Foreword   vi
Series Introduction   xi
Introduction   xiii

1 Understanding the policy context for teaching
   14–19 year olds   1
2 Understanding 14–19 provision   11
3 Preparing to teach 14–19 students – getting it
   right first time   22
4 Effective teaching of the 14–16 group   32
5 Effective teaching of the 16–19 group   42
6 Effective teaching of the 14–19 mixed-age group   48
7 Keys to effective teaching of 14–19 students   57
8 Sharpening your teaching skills – continuing
   professional development   65
9 Summary – effective teaching of 14–19 students
   in FE   75

   References and further reading   87
   Appendix: webpage resources   92
   Name Index   95
   Subject Index   97

Series Foreword

In the autumn of 1974, a young woman newly arrived from Africa landed in Devon to embark on a new life in England. Having travelled halfway round the world, she still longed for sunny Zimbabwe. Not sure what career to follow, she took a part-time job teaching EFL to Finnish students. Enjoying this, she studied thereafter for a PGCE at the University of Nottingham in Ted Wragg's Education Department. After teaching in secondary schools, she returned to university in Cambridge, and, having graduated, took a job in ILEA in 1984 in adult education. She loved it: there was something about adult education that woke her up, made her feel fully alive, newly aware of all the lifelong learning journeys being followed by so many students and staff around her. The adult community centre she worked in was a joyful place for diverse multi-ethnic communities. Everyone was cared for, including 90 year olds in wheelchairs, toddlers in the crèche, ESOL refugees, city accountants in business suits and university level graphic design students. In her eyes, the centre was an educational ideal, a remarkable place in which, gradually, everyone was helped to learn to be who they wanted to be. This was the Chequer Centre, Finsbury, EC1, the 'red house', as her daughter saw it, toddling in from the crèche. And so began the story of a long interest in further education that was to last for many years . . . why, if they did such good work for so many, were FE centres so under-funded and unrecognized, so under-appreciated?

It is with delight that, 32 years after the above story began, I write the Foreword to *The Essential FE Toolkit*, Continuum's new book series of 24 books on further education (FE) for teachers and college leaders. The idea behind the *Toolkit* is to provide a comprehensive guide to FE in a series of compact, readable books. The suite of 24 individual books are gathered together to provide the practitioner with an overall FE toolkit in specialist, fact-filled volumes designed to be easily accessible, written by experts with significant knowledge and experience in their individual fields. All of the authors have in-depth understanding of further education. But, 'Why is further education important? Why does it merit a whole series to be written about it?' you may ask.

At the Association of Colleges Annual Conference in 2005, in a humorous speech to college principals, John Brennan said that, whereas in 1995 further education was a 'political backwater', by 2005 FE had become 'mainstream'. John recalled that, since 1995, there had been '36 separate government or government-sponsored reports or White Papers specifically devoted to the post-16 sector'. In our recent regional research report (2006) for the Learning and Skills Development Agency, my co-author Yvonne Hillier and I noted that it was no longer 'raining policy' in FE, as we had described earlier (Hillier and Jameson 2003): there is now a torrent of new initiatives. We thought, in 2003, that an umbrella would suffice to protect you. We'd now recommend buying a boat to navigate these choppy waters, as it looks as if John Brennan's 'mainstream' FE, combined with a tidal wave of government policies, will soon lead to a flood of new interest in the sector, rather than end anytime soon.

There are good reasons for all this government attention on further education. In 2004/5, student numbers in LSC council-funded further education increased to 4.2m, total college income was around £6.1 billion, and the average college had an annual turnover of £15m. Further education has rapidly increased in national significance regarding the need for ever greater achievements in UK education and skills training for millions of learners, providing qualifications and workforce training to feed a UK national economy hungrily in competition with other OECD nations. The 120 recommendations of the Foster Review (2005) therefore in the main encourage colleges to focus their work on vocational skills, social inclusion and achieving academic progress. This series is here to consider all three of these areas and more.

The series is written for teaching practitioners, leaders and managers in the 572 FE/LSC-funded institutions in the UK, including FE colleges, adult education and sixth-form institutions, prison education departments, training and workforce development units, local education authorities and community agencies. The series is also written for PGCE/Cert Ed/City & Guilds Initial and continuing professional development (CPD) teacher trainees in universities in the UK, USA, Canada, Australia, New Zealand and beyond. It will also be of interest to staff in the 600 Jobcentre Plus providers in the UK and to many private training organizations. All may find this series of use and interest in learning about FE educational practice in the 24 different areas of these specialist books from experts in the field.

Our use of this somewhat fuzzy term 'practitioners' includes staff in the FE/LSC-funded sector who engage in professional practice in governance, leadership, management, teaching, training, financial and administration services, student support services, ICT and MIS technical support, librarianship, learning resources, marketing, research and development, nursery and crèche services, community and business support, transport and estates management. It is also intended to include staff in a host of other FE services including work-related training, catering, outreach and specialist health, diagnostic additional learning support, pastoral and religious support for students. Updating staff in professional practice is critically important at a time of such continuing radical policy-driven change, and we are pleased to contribute to this nationally and internationally.

We are also privileged to have an exceptional range of authors writing for the series. Many of our series authors are renowned for their work in further education, having worked in the sector for thirty years or more. Some have received OBE or CBE honours, professorships, fellowships and awards for contributions they have made to further education. All have demonstrated a commitment to FE that makes their books come alive with a kind of wise guidance for the reader. Sometimes this is tinged with world-weariness, sometimes with sympathy, humour or excitement. Sometimes the books are just plain clever or a fascinating read, to guide practitioners of the future who will read these works. Together, the books make up a considerable portfolio of assets for you to take with you through your journeys in further education. We hope the experience of reading the books will be interesting, instructive and pleasurable and that experience gained from them will last, renewed, for many seasons.

It has been wonderful to work with all of the authors and with Continuum's UK Education Publisher, Alexandra Webster, on this series. The exhilarating opportunity of developing such a comprehensive toolkit of books probably comes once in a lifetime, if at all. I am privileged to have had this rare opportunity, and I thank the publishers, authors and other contributors to the series for making these books come to life with their fantastic contributions to FE.

Dr Jill Jameson
Series Editor
March, 2006

Series Introduction

THE ESSENTIAL FE TOOLKIT SERIES

Jill Jameson
Series Editor

Introductions to Books for Lecturers

Guide to Teaching 14–19 – James Ogunleye

James Ogunleye introduces this valuable new guide on teaching 14–19 year olds in further education by explaining that this book is 'written by the teacher for the teacher'. He observes that a coordinated blend of 'knowledge, confidence and passion' (KCP) in 14–19 teaching, including good lesson planning/preparation, reflection about and professional development for your own teaching, are 'key to effective lesson delivery'. James encourages lecturers to 'join up' these aspects of successful teaching in creative and original ways, to benefit learners in the uniquely important age group of 14–19 learners. For this age group, it is vital that teachers try to 'get it right first time' to support and encourage the engagement and retention of learners, particularly more challenging students who are vulnerable to motivational problems and personal difficulties during adolescence.

James comments that the 'debate in the UK about how best to educate 14–19 year olds is unlikely to go away anytime soon'. These two contexts – practical teaching techniques for classroom lecturers in FE and the ongoing complex 14–19 policy debates in further education – are interwoven in useful, thought-provoking ways throughout this book. There are already a number of policy-focused books and journal articles on 14–19 developments, and also numerous practical teaching books. However, these two important strands of policy and practice are seldom woven together creatively for 14–19 teaching in the specific context of further education, linked directly to original case study information for FE lecturers. In this, James provides us with an unusual and informative guide.

I remember teaching students in the 14–19 age group myself in the 1970s, notably in Northamptonshire on Friday afternoons for English Lit (!). In that era, such a useful practitioners' guide as this was not available for teachers, especially for newly trained practitioners and those still building confidence and skill. The teachers of 14–19 year olds in FE today who read this book are therefore fortunate to have the benefit of James's many years of experience, research and skilled observations of successful teaching sessions in FE.

James provides a guide to enable lecturers to become familiar with the range of academic and vocational qualifications available to 14–19 year old students. The book gives an overview of the current and recent national agenda for 14–19 education and training, including the reform of qualifications, provision of academic and vocational subjects and the way in which schools and FE work together to o?er a broad range of 14–19 curricula. The book is informed by the results of authentic teaching techniques tested not only by James himself but also by the teachers and researchers who contributed to his research on this age group.

James also provides readers with illuminating insights into 14–19 year olds' views about teaching and learning in FE and he summarises the key attributes of successful teachers, as a basis for lecturers to develop their own effective teaching styles and techniques, including the use of starter activities, questioning, variable teaching styles, ICT and learning resources. James encourages lecturers to take active ownership of their own professional development as key to improving teaching practice. Finally, he leaves us with a useful set of information and publications resources for follow-up work in the References and Appendix. This practically focused, evidence-informed perceptive book by James Ogunleye will be essential reading for teachers of 14–19 year olds in FE for a long time to come, and I thoroughly commend it to you.

Dr Jill Jameson
Director of Research
School of Education and Training
University of Greenwich
j.jameson@gre.ac.uk

Introduction

This introduction explains the context for teaching 14–19 year olds in further education (FE) colleges. It highlights the ongoing partnerships between schools and FE colleges and presents an example of school–college provision for 14–16 year olds that may well represent a future model of 14–19 provision in FE. It concludes with a brief summary of explanation of the rest of the chapters in this book.

Context for teaching 14–19 in FE

Teaching 14–19 year olds is not the same as teaching mature students. Our knowledge of the theories of pedagogy and andragogy suggests that the two groups of students learn differently. According to the theory of andragogy (Knowles 1975, 1984; Cantor 1992; Cranton 1992), adult learners come to education with 'accumulated' life experiences that provide the basis for their learning. Adults are autonomous learners, self-directed and goal-oriented and are more willing to take responsibility for their learning decisions than are younger learners. Teachers of adult learners see their primary role as 'facilitators' of learning, negotiating and devolving decisions on learning activities to students. They use teaching methods that place emphasis on process over content. Pedagogic theory relates to the teaching of younger learners; it is teacher-focused and teacher-directed. Teachers take responsibility for decisions about what is learned, how it is learned and when it is learned; they use teaching methods that emphasize content over process. Other theories such as 'scaffolding' (or Vygotskian theory) draw on andragogy and pedagogy theories. Scaffolding theory 'accepts' students from where they are currently in their learning; it recognizes and acknowledges students' experience and 'builds to what is further from their

experience' (see Wilhelm, Baker and Dube 2001). Scaffolding theory is said to have practical application in 14–19 learning, in that,
although 14–19 learners need a great deal of structured support,
this can be provided within a context in which, gradually, teachers
encourage learners to take increasingly greater amounts of self-
directed learning over their years of 14–19 maturation so that
ultimately they become capable of independent self-directed
learning in a lifelong context in moving on to HE at 19.

Schools and colleges of further education explained

The UK education system is made up of compulsory and post-
compulsory education. Compulsory education takes place in the
school sector, which comprises primary and secondary schools;
post-compulsory education takes place in the further education
and higher education sectors. The further education sector comprises sixth-form colleges, general further education colleges, adult
and community education institutions, training providers, prison
education and specialist colleges.

The school sector

The school sector comprises the independent schools and the
grant-maintained schools. The grant-maintained schools have a
statutory duty to educate children from ages 5 to 16. They are
required by law to follow a common curriculum, otherwise known
as the National Curriculum. The National Curriculum was established by the Education Reform Act 1988, to enable grant-
maintained schools in England to teach the same courses, achieve
consistency and balance in teaching and learning across schools and
to raise standards. The Qualifications and Curriculum Authority
(QCA) in England, a quango, is charged with the formulation and
monitoring of the national curriculum while the government sets
the policy framework.

Organization of the National Curriculum

The National Curriculum is organized into four key stages or 'blocks of years', if we exclude the foundation stage. The following are the four key stages of the National Curriculum:

Key Stage 1 is taught in primary schools to pupils aged 5 to 7
Key Stage 2 is taught in primary schools to pupils aged 7 to 11
Key Stage 3 is taught in secondary schools to pupils aged 11 to 14
Key Stage 4 is taught in secondary schools to pupils aged 14 to 16

Core National Curriculum subjects at Key Stage 4 are English, maths, science, information and communication technology, physical education and citizenship. Non-core National Curriculum subjects include religious education, careers education and sex education. There are additional optional subjects from which students may choose – these include business studies, geography, history, music, art, leisure and tourism, child care and development and health and social care. At the end of Key Stage 4, most pupils will sit external examinations. Key Stage 4 provision has undergone a series of reforms in recent years, the latest of which is known as the Increased Flexibility Programme (IFP), which is discussed in chapter 1.

FE colleges

Further education, according to Frankel and Reeves (1996: 6), is 'situated in the social structure somewhere between the compulsory school sector on the one hand and industry and higher education on the other'. FE is made up of sixth-form and general further education colleges, adult and community institutions, training providers, prison education and specialist colleges such as agriculture and creative arts. The sector is the largest of the three sectors of English education system – school, further education and higher education sector. According to DfES (2005), 4.1 million learners were funded by the Learning and Skills Councils in the FE sector, the funding agency for further education in 2003/4, a majority of whom were adults, over 19 years of age. FE has a high proportion of 16–19 students in sixth forms – more than the number of 16–19 year olds in schools' sixth forms. Cantor, Roborts and Pratley (1995) describe the FE sector as a hotbed of qualifications – at one point it offered more than 17,000 qualifications, a quarter of which were in vocational areas (FEFC 1997). Unlike the secondary school sector, which has Kitemark qualifications such as GCSEs, students in FE study for qualifications as diverse as NVQ level 1, GCE A level, BTEC diplomas, accounting technicians' qualifications and foundation degrees, to mention but a few. Students in FE may enrol on courses that do not lead to a qualification, but do so out of interest in the subject. Teaching and learning styles/approaches in FE are distinctively different from the secondary sector – teaching methods in FE tend to be student-centred and students are encouraged to take responsibility for their learning.

Collaboration in 14–19 provision

Schools and FE colleges are increasingly working together to deliver learning to 14–16 year olds and enhance Key Stage 4 provision. A survey by the Learning and Skills Development Agency (LSDA 2002) in Nottinghamshire demonstrates the different forms that current 14–16 provision takes in colleges. Some programmes are linked to work experience, some are designed to give young people a 'foretaste' of practical experience in a college setting, some are offered discretely for largely excluded pupils to have 'an education experience' (p. 9); some programmes are offered on an ad hoc basis, designed to raise young people's low self-confidence and self-expectations. Another study by the Association of Colleges (Norrington and Hayday 2002) gave similar insights into further education colleges' contribution to the delivery of 14–16 programmes. They include, among others, the complete delivery of some Years 10 and 11 vocational subjects, and basic skills. The benefit of collaborative work between schools and colleges is evident in the range of Key Stage 4 courses on offer, which cover academic and vocational subjects, and key skills (see Ofsted 2003b). Pupils are generally positive about their college experiences and particularly cherish 'being treated like an adult' (Sproson 2003: 20; Ogunleye and McNay 2005). Pupils benefit from college teaching and learning resources, such as specialist suites for practical-oriented courses; they also welcome college emphasis on differentiated teaching and learning styles that meet their individual preferences. 'Good teamwork (between school teachers and college lecturers) further contributes to success when it ensures that staff have common expectations of pupil work and behaviour, and share strategies for managing behaviour' (Norrington and Hayday 2002: 19).

A model of school–college partnership

In September 2003, a new approach to delivering 14–16 provision was piloted in East London with the launch of a college-based centre for 14–16 provision, to educate a hundred Year 10 pupils displaced as a result of the closure of their school in the summer of 2003. The school had just emerged from special measures which had been in place for two years until just prior to the closure. The pilot project was as a result of a partnership between the local education authority and the local FE college; it is part of a drive by the LEA to raise standards of attainment and staying-on rates among young people in the borough. The centre offered the pupils all their KS4 national curriculum entitlements and a range of vocational options unavailable if they had continued their education in their former school. It is hoped that a seamless one-stop shop provision for 14–19 will provide a psychological lever for pupils in the borough to stay on in education till age 19, and a ladder for progression.

Brief summary explanation of chapters 1–9

Chapter 1 presents an overview of the contemporary national agenda for 14–19 education and training. It discusses a raft of government policy documents on 14–19 education and training, the importance of the 14–19 phase in the national drive to 'reskill' 'UK plc' and the need to achieve coherence in the 14–19 curriculum and qualifications framework following widespread criticisms of Curriculum 2000. The reform of 14–19 education and training was needed not only to ensure that young people have access to a wide range of academic and vocational curricula, but also to ensure that they leave school or college with requisite skills, knowledge and qualifications needed to do higher studies or go into work.

Chapter 2 examines 14–19 provision in FE in the light of the rolling reforms in the 14–19 education and training phase – particularly in relation to the provision of academic and vocational subjects. An academic curriculum is offered mainly in schools while a vocational curriculum is offered mainly in FE colleges, but the two sectors – school and FE – worked together to offer a broad range of academic and vocational curricula to 14–19 year olds. This chapter also highlights the diversity in the range of qualifications available to young learners in secondary schools and FE colleges; long gone are the days when the qualifications menu was limited to A level academic subjects. Resources permitted, 14–19 year olds now have the opportunity to 'pick and mix' and, in some cases, sample courses before they decide on which course they really want to do.

Chapter 3 provides readers with a rare insight into 14–19 year olds' views about teaching and learning in FE to underline a view that this group of learners deserves to be taught very well. It highlights three characteristics of lesson planning/preparation – knowledge, confidence and passion – as key to effective lesson delivery. It explains the need for a creative lesson plan within the context of teaching for creativity, pointing out key features of a creative lesson plan. It points out the importance of learning materials and teaching aids as 'enhancers' of student learning as well as the challenge of finding and selecting the right teaching aids appropriate for any planned lesson. It challenges lecturer to 'turn every lesson into an exciting classroom experience for the students'.

Chapter 4 highlights key attributes of successful teachers of 14–16 year olds as a basis for developing effective teaching styles and techniques. Successful teachers of 14–16 year olds helped students to make the transition from school to college; they made students see the point of coming to college for vocational learning; they made it a duty to meet with students prior to their first lesson; and, more importantly, they liked to take the creative challenge. This chapter also discusses a range of teaching techniques drawn from my work and those of others on 14–16 provision that can be applied or used in a range of teaching situations. Among the suggested techniques are creative lesson introduction, good teacher questioning skills and variable teaching styles.

Chapter 5 expands on a number of teaching techniques discussed in chapter 4. Techniques such as questioning, variable teaching styles and the use of ICT are key to effective teaching of 16–19 year olds. In examining these techniques, this chapter reinforces a central theme of this book: that effective teaching methods/practices are key to sustaining students' interest in lessons.

Chapter 6 examines a somewhat challenging aspect of FE teachers' work – teaching a mixed class of 14–19 year olds. It puts forward an example of a situation in which a lecturer might be required to teach a mixed-age lesson and highlights key techniques that can be used or applied in a variety of teaching situations. Teaching a mixed-age class requires good preparation and planning, as well as nurturing your ability as a lecturer to deliver lessons at different levels and paces across the age divide.

Chapter 7 presents the results of a study on teaching and learning in further education. The findings provide insights into students' and teachers' classroom behaviours and practices, as well as underlining the importance of knowing about these dispositions in your strive for excellence in teaching.

Chapter 8 points out the importance of professional development as key to improving teaching practice. It encourages lecturers to take an active interest in their professional development, noting that, despite FE colleges' best intentions, constraints of resources – money in particular – have often made it difficult to turn best intentions into reality. It explains why you need to draw up your own personal and professional development plan; to write up and update the plan year after year as your needs develop or change. It suggests ways in which you can develop yourself – such as becoming an examiner in your subject to gain insight into the marking process and to pick up useful tips for your students.

Chapter 9 summarizes some of the main teaching techniques, ideas and suggestions discussed throughout this book.

This book is written by the teacher for the teacher to use a familiar expression. I hope you benefit from reading the book, which derives from a number of years of experience of the 14–19 education phase, either as a Key Stage 4 teacher, sixth-form teacher, FE teacher or as a researcher on 14–19 education and training.

Finally, I will recommend that you check out the section on further reading and webpage resources as listed in the References and Appendix.

Unless otherwise stated all quotes (students' and teachers' comments) used throughout in this book were taken from Ogunleye (2002: 161–90).

1 Understanding the policy context for teaching 14–19 year olds

Introduction

The debate in the UK about how best to educate 14–19 year olds is unlikely to go away anytime soon. 14–19 education and training remains a priority of the current Labour government and the policy seemed to have concentrated the minds of both school and college leadership in recent years. This chapter provides enough information you need to know about government policy in relation to 14–19 year olds. It begins with an overview of the contemporary national agenda for 14–19 education and training. It highlights the rationale for the reform of 14–19 provision, noting in particular the economic argument for 'reskilling' the United Kingdom. It examines key government White Papers on 14–19 as well as initiatives – such as the Increased Flexibility programme and 14–19 Pathfinders – that flow from them. The chapter concludes with a review of the Tomlinson Report and the government's response to it.

Making the case for reform

The last eight years of the new Labour government have seen a raft of policy announcements, consultative papers and documents on education and training in England. Nowhere has the reform been so intensive as in initially post-16 provision, and lately 14–19. The government's case for reform of education and training has a recurrent theme – the need to underpin the nation's economy with the highly skilled workforce needed to raise national productivity and external competitiveness.

One reason for reform of 14–19 education and training is the need to end the arbitrary demarcation by age that has been built into 14–19 provision. At present, post-primary education is divided largely into 11–16, 16–19 and post-19. There is therefore a perception among young people that formal education ends at age 16 and that continuing in education is desirable, but not essential. Another reason for reform is the need to address a general rising disaffection and falling engagement with education and training among many young people. This disaffection is caused, in part, by young people's perception that the learning programmes arranged for them are irrelevant to real life (as I have argued elsewhere). Young people are unwilling to engage with education and training because of low achievement rates at 16, at which age only half of the school leavers in England achieve five or more good GCSE passes or the equivalent vocational qualifications, while 5 per cent leave schools with no GCSE passes. This low attainment in prior learning results in high drop-out rates in 16–19 education and training, according to a study by the Audit Commission/Ofsted (1993).

The twin factors of economic exigencies and a low skills base in comparison with other OECD member nations, against which the UK ranks 25th out of 29 for participation among young people in education (DfES 2003a), have augmented the case for reform of the 14–19 phase. There is, in the UK government's view, a sense of national urgency to raise productivity and improve the skills base of the national economy by ensuring that 'the skills, benefits of [the] education system match the needs of the knowledge economy' (Morris 2002: 5). This statement by Estelle Morris was underpinned by the recent White Paper *21st Century Skills: Realising Our Potential* (DfES 2003b), which places the reform of the 14–19 phase within the wider national skills development agenda.

The ongoing policy of widening participation is one means through which the government currently addresses the nation's skill shortages – especially at the technician level – by setting expansion targets of 50 per cent of young people under the age of 30 to have experience of higher education by 2010. This may include many on the work-based route from modern apprenticeships to foundation degree (Ainley 2003). However, key questions have been raised about the empirical basis of the 50 per cent targets (Kingston 2003), and about where these students will come from, since the targets rest on the assumption that a market exists for under 30s whose demand for education has not been met (Hodgson and Spours 2002). We could observe here that in South-east

England and Scotland the average participation rates are above 50 per cent.

Highlights of reform policies on 14–19 provision

The first White Paper on the 14–19 phase in England was published in 1996 by the Conservative government. *Learning to Compete: Education and Training for 14–19 Year Olds* (DfEE 1996b) sets the agenda that is now being amplified. *Learning to Compete* aimed to increase participation, attainment and progression into further/higher education and work (DfEE 1996b). The dearth of vocational options in the 14–16 curriculum relevant to pupils' particular needs was highlighted in the White Paper, following the publication of a consultative paper, *Equipping Young People for Working Life* (DfEE 1996a). The government sought to reform learning programmes by encouraging 14–16 year olds to study vocational subjects offered in schools or through some forms of partnership or collaborative work with further education colleges, training providers and employers. Other issues addressed in *Learning to Compete* include the perennial problems of underachievement, retention and low motivation for learning among young people, especially some subgroups such as white working-class males and Caribbean males.

The Labour government's consultative/policy documents on 14–19 education and training since *Learning to Compete* have sought to achieve a structural reform of 14–19 provision. In *Schools Achieving Success* (DfES 2001), the government emphasized the main thrusts of *Learning to Compete* as well as addressing factors limiting coherence in the 14–19 phase. The government proposed to achieve 'high quality', widely recognized vocational options for young people and encouraged parity of esteem, however it is defined, between academic and vocational qualifications. It sought to encourage creativity in learning programmes by 'creating space in the 14–16 curriculum to allow students to pursue their talents and aspiration, while maintaining a strong focus on the basics' (DfES 2001: 30). I have argued the case for fostering creativity in learning programmes for young people elsewhere.

The introduction of GCSEs in vocational subjects from September 2002 (widely available from September 2003) was a key plank of the proposals on vocational education in *Schools Achieving Success*. The new GCSEs are underpinned by work-related learning that is clearly focused and more relevant to individual learners' needs.

Like traditional GCSEs, the new GCSEs emphasize knowledge to ensure that these qualifications gain the confidence of young people and stakeholders such as higher education institutions and employers. There is a recognition that schools alone may not be adequately resourced or have sufficient expertise or institutional capacity to offer vocational courses to young people without effective partnerships with other stakeholders. The government, therefore, anticipates more collaborative work between schools, colleges of further education, training providers and employers of labour, to ensure that such courses are delivered by teachers with vocational expertise using industry-standard facilities. This is particularly important in subjects in which access to high standards of technical expertise and specialist facilities feature as a major component of coursework (e.g. construction, engineering, hair and beauty).

The government's most recent White Paper on 14–19 provision, *Opportunity and Excellence* (DfES 2003a), embodies plans already set out in *Schools Achieving Success*. In *Opportunity and Excellence* the government amplified plans to achieve a coherent 14–19 phase by effecting immediate changes to the contents of the National Curriculum, in which schools will be allowed to 'disapply' pupils from particular National Curriculum subjects at Key Stage 4. The Qualifications and Curriculum Authority was tasked to introduce and develop new 'hybrid' GCSEs to encourage greater take-up of general and vocational studies within the context of the Increased Flexibility Programme (see below). The government also removed the historical distinction between general and vocational GCSE subjects, 'and their respective labels' (DfES 2003a: 24). Other policy emphases in *Opportunity and Excellence* include requirements on schools to provide work-related and enterprise learning in programmes for 14–16, informed by the recommendations in Davies's (2002) review of enterprise in education. The review identified gaps in students' business knowledge and financial skills, caused by the paucity of enterprise learning in programmes for young people in schools and colleges; it recommends that the National Curriculum include subjects or units on enterprise. This twin requirement on schools to provide work-related and enterprise learning in

14–16 programmes would not necessarily require additional curriculum time, according to Schools Minister David Miliband (see Miliband 2003). Miliband's optimism was obviously based on the work of a number of 14–19 Pathfinders set up by the government following the Green Paper *14–19: Extending Opportunities, Raising Standards* (DFES 2002) to test the variety of collaborative delivery models for 14–19 provision (see below).

Increased Flexibility Programme

The Increased Flexibility Programme (IFP) was rolled out nationwide in England in 2002. It was initially a two-year programme (2002–4), but it looks set to continue into the future. IFP introduced a range of new GCSEs in applied and vocational subjects to Key Stage 4 provision, as part of a national drive to broaden the range of curricula available to 14–16 year olds and to raise staying-on rates in education and training after 16. The programme is delivered through partnerships between FE colleges, schools, local education authorities and employers. Under the IF programme, Key Stage 4 students can take vocational lessons in FE college for up to two days a week; vocational learning under IFP may include work experience programmes at any stage of Years 10 and 11. Since its introduction in 2002, the IFP has 'expanded to second, third and fourth cohorts commencing in the autum term of each of the years 2003, 2004 and 2005. For each cohort, about 300 partnerships have supported the learning of around 40,000 young people in Years 10 and 11' (Golden *et al.* 2005: iv).

14–19 Pathfinders

You might be forgiven if you think this paragraph is going to be discussing map reading – certainly not! The term *14–19 Pathfinders* is one of the recent additions to the 14–19 lexicon which FE practitioners may have to get used to. The scheme is part of the government's 14–19 reform agenda; it was first set out in the Green Paper *14–19: Extending Opportunities, Raising*

Standards (DfES 2002). It aimed to test how local partners collaborate to deliver the 14–19 education and training phase in a variety of settings. Thirty-nine pathfinders were set up between January and September 2003. An evaluation of the 39 pathfinders carried out by the University of Leeds on behalf of the Department for Education and Skills showed that in September 2003 '*all* pathfinders reported expected or better than expected progress on collaboration and on offering a broader curriculum' (Higham *et al.* 2004: 21).

The Tomlinson Report

In September 2004, Sir Mike Tomlinson, former chief inspector of the school inspectorate, Ofsted, published the final Report of his inquiry into the qualification and curriculum arrangements of 14–19 education and training in England. A key aim of the 14–19 Reform Group – as it is formally known – was to address the problems of fragmentation, transparency and 'too many titles' in the existing 14–19 qualification structure and the particular problem of 'over-examined' pupils. The Report sets out a number of proposals designed to offer a new rationale for the 14–19 curriculum and qualifications 'within a diploma framework, where progression routes and the value of qualifications are clear' (The Tomlinson Report 2004: para 1). The Report proposed a unified framework of diplomas which, over time, will replace the existing plethora of qualifications (table 1.1). Qualifications such as GCE, AVCE, GCSE, VGCSE and NVQ will become component parts of the new diplomas' framework. The diplomas will be available in four levels comprising entry diplomas, foundation diplomas, intermediate diplomas and advanced diplomas. The four levels collectively will attract a minimum of 720 credits – divided between 480 credits for main learning and 240 credits for core learning. Each level will attract a minimum of 180 credits – divided in the proportion of 120 credits for main learning and 60 credits for core learning. Attainment of minimum credits of 180 will contribute towards the next level. For example, the attainment of minimum credits of 180 at entry level will contribute towards foundation diplomas;

attainment of minimum credits of 180 at foundation level will contribute towards intermediate diplomas, and so on.

Dividing the credits between two learning programmes – core learning and main learning – underlines the emphasis the 14–19 Reform Group placed on the relevancy of the curriculum and the different expectations from the teaching of it. Core learning will enable students to develop the 'generic' skills and knowledge needed to prepare them for higher education, while main learning will enable students to develop 'knowledge, skills and understanding' of academic and vocational subjects and disciplines which provide a basis 'for work-based training, higher education and employment' (para 4). Core learning areas will include functional maths, ICT, communication skills, an extended essay and 'wider activities' such as work experience. Students will have to pass the core learning subjects to pass the diploma. The Report envisaged that the diplomas' framework will be flexible enough to allow students to enter it at 14 and progress through the 14–19 phase.

The Tomlinson Report was widely welcomed by teachers and a majority of the education establishment (Curtis 2004); there was a view that the country may have found a way to address, among other things, the twin problem of transparency in 14–19 qualifications and relevancy of the curriculum framework. However, the Report was criticized by a small but powerful section of the press over its proposal to replace GCSEs and A levels – traditionally, A levels were regarded as the 'gold standard' qualifications for gaining entrance to higher education in England.

The government's response to the Tomlinson Report

The government, in its response, agreed broadly with many of the proposals in the Tomlinson Report – for example, the need to achieve coherence in the 14–19 curriculum, the need to reduce the number of existing qualifications, the need to improve the status of vocational qualifications and the need for more employer involvement in designing the curriculum framework. The government also welcomed a proposal that students must achieve functional English and maths at level 2 to achieve a diploma at level 2. The government, however, rejected the main plank of the Tomlinson

Table 1.1 Outline of the Tomlinson Report diploma framework

Diplomas				Current qualifications
Advanced	Core	Main learning	Level 3	Advanced Extension Award; GCE and VCE AS and A level; level 3 NVQ; equivalent qualifications
Intermediate	Core	Main learning	Level 2	GCSE grades at A★–C; intermediate GNVQ; level 2 NVQ; equivalent qualifications
Foundation	Core	Main learning	Level 1	GCSE grades D–G; foundation GNVQ; level 1 NVQ; equivalent qualifications
Entry	Core	Main learning	Entry	Entry-level certificates and other work below level 1

Source: The Tomlinson Report (2004).

Report – a recommendation that existing GCSEs and A levels be replaced as free-standing qualifications. The government made it clear in the *14–19 Education and Skills* White Paper (DfES 2005: para 6) that it will 'retain GCSEs and A levels as cornerstones of' any future 14–19 qualification frameworks. The government rejected another of Tomlinson's recommendations: that academic and vocational qualifications be aligned into a single qualifications framework. Instead, the government proposed distinctive, three-level occupation-specific diplomas that will include academic and vocational learning (table 1.2). The diplomas will be introduced in 14 occupation areas and will become a national entitlement by 2015. The 14 'lines' of diplomas will be phased in, with the first four diplomas – in health and social care, information and communication technology, engineering, and creative and media studies – available in 2008.

Conclusion

The raft of government policy documents on 14–19 education and training in the last eight years of the Labour government can only

Table 1.2 A new system of specialized diplomas

Level	Qualifications	Learning contents	
3	Advanced	Academic and vocational material	*Learners must have functional English and maths to achieve a diploma at level 2*
2	GCSE	Academic and vocational material	
1	Foundation	Academic and vocational material	

demonstrate one thing – the importance of the 14–19 phase in the national drive to 'reskill' UK plc. But more importantly it demonstrates the urgent need to achieve coherence in the 14–19 curriculum and qualifications frameworks following widespread criticisms of the Curriculum 2000 initiative (see Hodgson and Spours 2005). The reform of 14–19 education and training is needed not only to ensure that young people have access to a wide range of academic and vocational curricula, but also to ensure that they leave school or college with the requisite knowledge, qualifications and skills needed to do higher studies or go into work. Schemes such as the Increased Flexibility Programme were introduced by the government as a means through which vocational aspects of 14–16 provision were delivered. It has enabled Key Stage 4 students to access quality vocational and work-related learning outside the school environment. 14–19 Pathfinders, another government initiative, was set up to test how local partners such as schools, colleges, local education authorities and employers collaborate to deliver the 14–19 education and training phase.

Sir Mike Tomlinson's landmark Report was widely seen as a serious attempt to achieve coherence in the 14–19 education and training phase. The Report proposed the streamlining of 14–19 curriculum and qualifications structure in order to meet Britain's skills need in the twenty-first century. However, a key Tomlinson's recommendation that GCSEs and A levels be replaced as standalone qualifications was rejected by the government. In rejecting this recommendation, the government argued that the GCSEs and A levels must be the 'cornerstone' of any new system. Instead of creating an overarching diploma in the 14–19 phase, the government proposed three-level occupational-specific diplomas in 14 subject areas that will become a national entitlement by 2015. Four of the 14 lines of diplomas will be introduced in September 2008.

2 Understanding 14–19 provision

Introduction

This chapter examines 14–19 provision in FE in the light of the rolling reforms in the 14–19 education and training phase. It explains briefly the components of the Key Stage 4 curriculum in schools, contrasting it with the curriculum offered to 14–16 year olds in FE colleges. It highlights the division between academic and vocational curriculum and qualifications offered to 14–19 year olds, despite a national effort to develop a coherent curriculum and qualifications framework for this age group.

The Key Stage 4 curriculum has certain distinctive features. For all students it forms the last period of compulsory education; for some it will be end of formal education. During Key Stage 4, there is a transition between the compulsory curriculum of Key Stage 3 and the greater flexibility and choice post 16.

(QCA 2003: 5)

14–16 provision

If you are not familiar with the organization of secondary curriculum such as the provision for 14–16, your knowledge starts here. The provision for 14–16 year olds or Key Stage 4 curriculum is designed to meet the needs of students in Years 10 and 11 groups – students in the last two years of compulsory education. The Key Stage 4 curriculum is subject to the National Curriculum requirements, which set the number of compulsory subjects that students must study. There are three aspects to the Key Stage 4 curriculum – they are *core* elements, *entitlement* elements and *vocational* elements. Core National Curriculum subjects include English, English literature, mathematics, science, physical education, information and communications technology, religious education, sex education, careers education, citizenship and work-related learning. Subjects in the entitlement elements include design and technology, humanities and arts. Vocational elements of the Key Stage 4 curriculum are delivered within the context of the Increased Flexibility Programme. Under section 363 of the 1996 Education Act, schools may 'disapply' up to two National Curriculum subjects for any one student, if they take the view that the student will benefit from work-related learning or from the wide range of vocational subjects offered through partnerships with FE colleges and training providers. All academic and vocational subjects in 14–16 provision may be studied to GCSE level.

The academic and vocational curriculum at Key Stage 4
The Key Stage 4 curriculum is broadly academic. English, maths, science and ICT are generally regarded as subjects which have national and international significance, and which students must study. The government demonstrated the significance of these subjects recently by introducing new Key Stage 4 science and mathematics programmes of study effective from 2006 and 2008 respectively (QCA 2003; DfES 2005). From September 2006, the study of science at GCSE will be compulsory – in that it may not be disapplied – and students who intend to study science at A level may only do so if they have taken double science at Key Stage 4. Similarly, from September 2008, the study of functional mathematics will be compulsory and a prerequisite to achieving a diploma at level 2 under the new specialized diplomas framework discussed in chapter 1. The introduction of functional mathematics at Key Stage 4 followed Professor Adrian Smith's inquiry into post-14 mathematics education and Mike Tomlinson's review of the 14–19 curriculum and qualifications framework (Dfes 2004b; Tomlinson Report 2004). The vocational curriculum at Key Stage 4 is in an embryonic stage; vocational subjects range from travel and tourism, health and social care to business studies.

An example of Key Stage 4 curriculum arrangements

KS4 curriculum

All students in Years 10 and 11 follow the core curriculum, which includes:

English
mathematics
science
physical education
core studies

In addition to the core curriculum, students are able to choose from a range of options. Each student studies one subject from the following technology option GCSE courses:

ICT textiles
electronics
graphics & engineering, food technology, resistant materials
*art & design
*health & social care

In addition to the technology option, students choose three courses from the following list:

art, art & design
drama
music
Spanish
health & social care
humanities
history
geography
business studies
French
German
Urdu
RE

If either art & design or health & social care have been chosen from the technology options students will also have chosen it as one of the options from the above list.

Art & Design and Health & Social Care are double awards.
Source: www.banbury.oxon.sch.uk

The arrangements of curriculum at Key Stage 4 at Banbury School illustrates a view that the extent to which students can pick and mix subjects at Key Stage 4 is dependent on a school resource capability.

Key Stage 4 provision in FE
A major plank of the reform of Key Stage 4 curriculum in September 2003 was the flexibility given to schools to determine where learning takes place. This means part or all aspects of the Key Stage 4 curriculum can be delivered outside schools, in places such as further education colleges and in workplaces – so that students on vocational courses can be provided with the opportunity to do work experience. For the first time in recent years, collaborations between schools/LEAs, colleges and employers are actively encouraged by the government as part of a drive to develop a coherent work-relevant curriculum for 14–19 year olds. The partnerships between these stakeholders have led to a significant increase in the number of 14–16 year olds receiving all or part of their education in FE. According to the government's medium-term strategy for children and learners (DfES 2004a), by 2008 over 180,000 14–16 year olds will be studying vocational subjects – most of which will be delivered in FE colleges.

16–19 provision

The term *16–19 provision* is an ambiguous and all-compassing term. It is used to describe a specialist education for 16–19 year olds in the United Kingdom. 16–19 education in this context denotes qualifications system and the arrangements of curriculum, its content and delivery, to students aged 16–19 in school sixth forms, sixth-form colleges and general further education colleges. In recent years, curriculum provision for 16–19 year olds in work-related training or work-based learning such as modern apprenticeships was brought under the 16–19 provision in line with the government's drive to achieve a cohesive curriculum and qualifications system for all learners in the 16–19 education and training phase.

Academic and vocational curriculum in the 16–19 phase
The 16–19 academic curriculum is geared towards A level qualifications, which are divided into AS and A2 – advanced supplementaries and advanced level respectively. AS levels and A2 are theoretically comparable in standards, except that the content is half of those of A levels. Traditional science, arts and humanities subjects still form the bulk of academic curriculum offered to 16–19 year olds. The curriculum is made of course specifications or syllabuses written by the examination boards with the approval of the Qualifications and Curriculum Authority (QCA) in England and the Scottish Qualifications Authority (SQA). Academic courses attract a minority proportion of 16–19 year olds; this situation has led to a debate in the United Kingdom about the justification for committing so many resources – funds, etc. – to curriculum provision that 'serve the interest' of a minority of students.

The vocational certificates of education (VCEs) were introduced in schools and colleges in September 2000 to replace GNVQs. The VCEs were conceived as alternatives to traditional GCE A levels so that, for the purpose of university admissions, grades for VCEs will have equal standing as grades for GCEs. Students can take advanced subsidiary VCE (three units), advanced VCE (six units) and advanced VCE double award (12 units) in business, engineering and travel and tourism, among other courses. Assessment methods used for the AVCE are, to some extent, similar to those of the GNVQ. Students are assessed through externally moderated coursework; they are also assessed through external written tests in at least two units. In a marked departure from the multiple-choice format of the old GNVQ external tests, the AVCE external tests are believed to be more rigorous, more challenging and arguably more academic.

National Qualifications Framework

All qualifications in England are linked to the National Qualifications Framework (NQF), which sets out to 'help learners make informed decisions on the qualifications they need, by comparing the levels of different qualifications and identifying clear progression routes to their chosen career' (www.qca.org.uk). The main aims of the NQF are:

- to promote access, motivation and achievement in education and training, strengthening international competitiveness
- to promote lifelong learning by helping people to understand clear progression routes
- to avoid duplication and overlap of qualifications while making sure all learning needs are covered
- to promote public and professional confidence in the integrity and relevance of national awards

(source: www.qca.org.uk)

Table 2.1 shows three NQF levels in the 14–19 qualifications framework.

GNVQ intermediate

General vocational national qualification (GNVQ) intermediate is available until 2006. GNVQ intermediate is equivalent to four GCSE A*–C grades. The GNVQ was introduced in schools and colleges in 1992 by the National Council for Vocational Qualifications (NCVQ), now subsumed into the Qualifications and Curriculum Authority (QCA), to provide broad education 'both for training leading to employment, and for further and higher education' (NCVQ 1995: 5). Unlike the A level, which emphasizes content knowledge, the GNVQ lays emphasis on competent performance, while (arguably) content knowledge gets less priority (Green 1997). Also, unlike the traditional A level examinations, assessments generally take the form of observations of performance; assignment, project work and written evidence. The vocational system emphasizes development of general skills, knowledge and understanding and production of evidences (in the form of a student portfolio). Assessment in GNVQ has two broad grading themes, which are common to all units: process and quality. Process

Table 2.1   14–19 qualifications and the National Qualifications Framework

NQF level	General academic qualifications	General vocational qualifications	Vocationally related qualifications	Work-based qualifications
3	AS and A2 GCE	AVCE	OCR nationals; BTEC first diploma	NVQ level 3
2	GCSE – five or more A*–C grades	Vocational GCSEs (A*–C) (or GNVQ intermediate)	OCR level 2 national certificates; BTEC first certificates	NVQ level 2
1	GCSE – grades D–G	Vocational GCSEs grades D–G	OCR level 1 national; BTEC introductory certificates	NVQ level 1

includes planning, monitoring and evaluation; while quality denotes the quality of outcomes of students' work. The grading themes are 'designed to recognize and reward those students who consistently produce high-quality work above the standard requirement; demonstrate the process of planning, using information (research) and evaluating their work' (NCVQ 1995: 6). GNVQ is being phased out and replaced with AVCE.

The context for the 14–19 qualifications framework

The Dearing Report, published in 1996 (Dearing 1996), examined the pattern of qualifications for the 16–19 years age group. It divided qualifications into three categories: academic (A level), applied (GNVQ) and vocational (NVQ); this later provided the basis for developing Curriculum 2000 (DfEE 1997), which was introduced in schools, sixth-form colleges and general further education colleges in September 2000. The aims of the reforms were, among others, to make the post-16 (further) education curriculum broader and more flexible by encouraging students to mix and match academic and vocational subjects as appropriate.

Academic and vocational qualifications available to 14–19 year olds in FE

Academic and vocational qualifications for 14–19 year olds are external qualifications, defined in section 96 of the Learning and Skills Act 2000 as those qualifications awarded or authenticated by a 'person' other than the school, institution, employer or a member of their staff. External qualifications are therefore subject to approval and accreditation to the national qualifications framework by regulatory bodies such as the Qualifications and Curriculum Authority (QCA) and its Scottish equivalent, the Scottish Qualifications Authority (SQA). For an external qualification to be approved and accredited, the awarding body has to show that it meets a set of criteria which include a demonstration of 'high-quality standards'. The three unitary awarding bodies in England – AQA, Edexcel and OCR – offered academic and vocational qualifications which include GCSE, GCE and AVCE. Other awarding bodies such as City and Guilds offered vocational qualifications for particular occupational groups.

Academic and vocational qualifications available to 14–16 year olds

Traditionally, FE colleges do not normally offer academic courses to 14–16 year old students unless the students are in college by special arrangements or enrolled on 'dedicated' programmes in which English, maths, science and other core National Curriculum subjects are taught (see chapter 1). Where such arrangements or programmes exist, most students will be offered qualifications such as GCSEs for core National Curriculum subjects. Most qualifications available to 14–16 year olds in FE are vocationally related. At the time of writing, these qualifications include VGCSEs in applied art and design, applied business, applied ICT, applied science, engineering, health and social care, leisure and tourism, manufacturing, motor vehicle, food technology, hospitality, performing arts, media and public services. Equivalent qualifications such as NVQ level 2 and BTEC first certificates are available in most of these areas.

As a lecturer, you will need to familiarize yourself with the relevant course specifications to know precisely what standards your pupils are expected to reach to gain requisite qualifications. Almost all the vocational subjects mentioned earlier can be delivered at level 1; you should therefore ensure that those students who have been entered for level 2 qualifications receive lessons appropriate to that level. If you are not sure about whether you are to deliver lessons to level 2, for example, check with your students' head of year in the local school for clarification. Your students will almost certainly feel hard done by if at the end of their study they were not entered for GCSE level qualification because of an error on your part.

Academic and vocational qualifications available to 16–19 year olds

If you have experience of teaching 16–19 year olds, the chances are that you are already familiar with the range of qualifications available to them. If you are new to teaching this age group, there is no better place than this book and its further references to familiarize yourself with the range of academic and vocational qualifications available to 16–19 year old students in FE. As you may have noticed in table 2.1, the two main qualifications taken by this age group are GCE A/AS level and AVCE. In other words, most 16–19 year olds in FE are likely to be doing one or both of the two groups of qualifications. The A level system of qualification emphasizes content knowledge and the use of examinations to test such knowledge. A levels are split into two parts under Curriculum 2000 – AS and A2 respectively. There are six modules in each course which can be taken over a two-year period. AS and A level qualifications are available in accounting, art, biology, business studies, chemistry, computing, drama, economics, English language, English literature, French, geography, German, graphics, history, information and communication technology, law, mathematics, philosophy, physics, psychology, sociology and media studies, statistics and critical thinking, among others. As earlier stated, the AVCE system of qualifications is an offshoot of GNVQ qualifications. AVCE is equivalent to A level; its development represents an attempt by the government to achieve so-called 'parity of esteem', in which these qualifications have the same currency or status. Although real 'parity of esteem' is a noble aim, it has not so far been achieved in reality; it remains a challenge for the government to change long-held perceptions of vocational qualifications as 'inferior' to academic qualifications. In addition to taking A level/AVCE courses, students are also required to study for separate qualification in at least one key skill such as application of number, communication and information and communication technology.

National Vocational Qualifications

The National Vocational Qualification (NVQ) is another main qualification available to 16–19 year old students in FE. The NVQ was set up principally to meet the needs of employers, but the qualification can also be used as a basis for applying to college or university for further education – although NVQs are not highly rated by admissions tutors in higher education. The NVQ adopts a competence-based approach to assessments and qualifications. This means that to gain an NVQ award, a candidate must provide evidence of how competent he or she is at performing a set of duties or prescribed tasks at work or, in some cases, in a simulated work environment, while meeting a set of (predetermined) performance criteria laid down by the relevant industry lead body (LB).

NVQs are available in a range of vocational areas, such as accounting, administration, customer service, construction, health, social care, child minding, hairdressing and beauty therapy. The purposes of the occupational standards are: 'to provide competent well-trained staff as a means of enhancing the effectiveness of the industry' and 'to recognize actual work performance with nationally recognized qualifications and develop the skills and knowledge necessary for effective performance' (NVQs flyers, Edexcel, February 1999). Candidates are assessed by observations of performance; by assignment, project work and simulation. Even though the emphasis is on competent performance, a number of accredited bodies (such as the Association of Accounting Technicians) are now assessing underpinning knowledge via 'Central Assessment' or 'External Examination'.

BTEC qualifications

You should also be familiar with BTEC qualifications, especially BTEC national certificates and diplomas. BTEC national certificates and diplomas are vocationally related qualifications that are well established in FE. In recent years, BTEC courses have increased in popularity among lecturers and curriculum leaders; an increasing number of students are being encouraged to take these courses as alternatives to AVCEs. BTEC qualifications are available in art and design, business, electronic engineering, IT practitioners, media production, music technology, performing arts and travel and tourism, among other occupational areas. A BTEC national diploma is equivalent to NVQ level 3 or 3 A levels.

Conclusion

You may have noticed from the foregoing paragraphs that the curriculum post-14 is grouped broadly into academic and vocational subjects. The academic curriculum is offered mainly in schools while the vocational curriculum is offered mainly in FE colleges. However, the two sectors – schools and FE colleges – work together to offer a broad range of academic and vocational curricula to learners in the 14–19 age group.

You may also have noticed the amount of diversity in the range of qualifications available to young learners in schools and FE colleges; long gone are the days when the qualifications menu was limited to A level academic subjects. Resources permitted, 14–19 year olds now have the opportunity to 'pick and mix' and, in some cases, sample courses before they decide which one they really want to do. As a lecturer, you need to stay on top of the curriculum developments in your subject; familiarize yourself thoroughly with the subject specification and ensure that you teach Key Stage 4 students at the right level of qualification, which is level 2 for those who are taking GCSEs. Also, you need to be familiar with the range of non-traditional qualifications available to students taking your subject to maximize their chances of doing well in the subject. The next chapter will show you how to prepare to teach your 14–19 year-olds to do well in your subject.

3 Preparing to teach 14–19 students – getting it right first time

Introduction

This chapter begins by providing you with a rare insight into 14–19 year olds' views about teaching and learning in FE to underline a view that this group of learners deserve to be taught very well. It highlights three characteristics of lesson planning and preparation – knowledge, confidence and passion – as key to effective lesson delivery. It explains the need for a creative lesson plan within the context of teaching for creativity, pointing out key features of a creative lesson plan. It discusses the role of learning materials and teaching aids as enhancers of student learning as well and the challenge of finding and selecting the right teaching aids appropriate for the planned lesson.

Insights into 14–19 year olds' enthusiasms for study in FE

Studies into teaching and learning experiences of 14–19 year olds in further education colleges by this author and others showed that students enjoyed being in college and were generally satisfied with the quality of teaching they received (Ogunleye and McNay 2005; Sproson 2003; Ogunleye 2002). Students believed they were learning; they also believed they were enjoying their courses; younger students, in particular, liked being treated like adults. Like a delicious ice cream the college environment tastes good in the mouths of most 14–19 year olds; they seemed to want more of it. Here is what a 15 year old had to say about his experience in an FE college:

When I came to this college, yeah, they give me support. They lifted my head high. My being here [in the college] has been beneficial – in my work, in my reading. All I've got is college and I will be nobody if I'm not here.

(Ogunleye and McNay 2005)

Many older students held the same views; they particularly cherished the independence and the sense of freedom that the college learning environment provides. As one student put it:

I feel that I have learnt a lot. I didn't really know anything before I came here. I am doing quite well. I prefer the atmosphere here, much more relaxed. You can do things in your own way; you have the independence.

(Natalie, NVQ administration in a sixth-form college,
South-east England)

I like the college because they give you more freedom; they let you do what you need to do. It is better than school. I feel that I'm learning.

(Semina, A level history in a North-east
England FE college)

Andrew, A level media studies in a North-east England FE college, enthused:

It's been pretty good. I have learnt quite a lot, especially things that I didn't know until I came to this college – I now know how to use a camera.

Tapping into students' enthusiasms

The previous paragraphs gave insights into why 14–19 year olds were enthusiastic about studying in FE; this provided what is essentially some baseline intelligence on the group of students you are about to teach. What is more pleasing to know than that you have won the confidence and admiration of your students even before they get to know you? But the key to tapping into students' enthusiasms lies in smart lesson planning and preparation, as this group of students can also easily get bored and frustrated if their lessons are not well-delivered. The following paragraphs highlight key characteristics of lesson planning and preparation.

It's all about KCP – knowledge, confidence and passion

Those three words say a lot about a teacher. There is little doubt that FE lecturers have specialist knowledge of their subjects. Students believe this too: an earlier study by this author showed that students regard FE lecturers as a reservoir of knowledge (Ogunleye 2002). There is also little doubt that lecturers have passion for their subjects and are confident about delivering their lectures. What is in doubt is whether lecturers fully appreciate the relationships between these three characteristics of lesson planning and presentation and whether they manifest them in lesson planning. Your self-confidence and passion for your subject will determine the extent of your lesson planning and preparation; it will make a difference in the way you design or structure your lesson plan, in the way you source, organize and write up teaching and learning materials and in the way you present your lesson.

Be confident

Confidence at all the stages of teaching and learning include being confident to deliver the subject, to use the teaching or instructional materials and to control or manage the class. In a study by Loyd *et al.* (2000: 353), teachers reported that their confidence fell across certain 'process skills' when they had a 'clearer appreciation' of the subject. Research by Davies (2000) found that teachers felt frustrated by their inability to keep on top of their knowledge and skills to make learning relevant to students' needs. Students can spot a teacher who lacks confidence delivering a particularly difficult topic, especially when the teacher's styles of delivery made them nod off in lesson. You must demonstrate ability to inspire to get the students to appreciate why they must learn a difficult topic. Joined-up thinking in KCP in lesson planning and preparation will enable you to anticipate aspects of the lesson that students are likely to find difficult. This kind of thinking will also enable you to prepare students beforehand by identifying and specifying possible 'turn-off' or 'nodding-off' points in lessons – by thinking through other ways of presenting difficult bits to students, with passion.

You can build your confidence in a number of ways. McFarlane (1993: 60) believed that you can acquire confidence in the lecturer's role by simply self-perpetuating it. This is particularly true for experienced lecturers, but less so for beginner teachers trying to cut their teeth in the profession. Whatever the stage you are in your career, you can build your confidence by maintaining an up to date knowledge of your subject as well as the skills you need to teach the subject.

One way to embed confidence in lesson planning and preparation is to dream about the kind of reaction you would expect from students momentarily as they file out of your class – wouldn't you want the students to feel that they have learned a lot in your class today, to vow (yes to vow) that they would not want to miss the next lesson for all the world? Students will *feel* they have learned a lot in your class and will *go out of their way* not to miss future lessons if you make it a habit to deliver an interesting lesson *most of the time*. What is more, you will earn the confidence of your students as someone who 'springs' surprises in lessons.

Be enthusiastic

Having the knowledge of the subject and being confident about delivering it may not achieve the desired outcome – enhancing student learning – if you have little enthusiasm for the subject. There is more to teaching 14–19 year olds than delivering a good lesson; teaching is also about influencing the next generation of teachers and professionals in other occupations. An enthusiasm for the subject you teach may encourage a younger learner to take a level 3 qualification in the subject, or it may encourage a 16–19 year old to explore the subject at university level.

Your students have come a long way in their schooling even before you first met them; it is important to instil in them positive impressions about education, especially for students who may have had poor experiences of education in the past. If you ask many 14–16 year olds in FE – especially the so-called 'difficult-to-manage' cohorts – their views about schooling, you will get a mixed bag of responses. You, therefore, have a responsibility to change the way they perceive learning. If you are not excited about the topic you are teaching, neither will your students be – and why should they? To turn the students on, you must first turn yourself on. Be passionate about the subject and make it genuinely come alive; above all, let your passion be contagious.

Tips on how to reflect your enthusiasm for your subject in lesson planning and preparation

Let your passion inform the way you write or organize learning material – do this by identifying potentially frustrating moments that are unavoidable in lessons. You can then plan in advance 'hook points' that can sustain students' interest. 'Hook points' in a lesson plan might include asking students individually questions on the background information search that you have asked them to collect in the previous lesson. Hook points might also include explaining technical terms and information. If you are teaching a mixed group of 14–19 students, ensure that students' activities in the lesson plan are structured in such a way that encourages students to build on previous knowledge, while differentiating between the needs of 14–16 year olds and 16–19 year olds.

Planning your lesson

We now come to the point where you need to turn your knowledge of the subject and your confidence and passion in delivering it into a truly creative lesson plan that will aid student learning of the subject. It is important to get the planning right first time, every time. Research by Pratt (1981) supports this age-old teacher wisdom – good lesson-planning aids lesson presentation. A lesson plan is like a road map – not an end in itself, but a means to it. Having a lesson plan does not necessarily guarantee a good delivery of lesson, but provides a formal structure for the lesson. Besides, it portrays the teacher in a good light – as someone who takes teacher professionalism very seriously. In recent time, a lesson plan and a scheme of work are key requisite documentation in Ofsted inspections in schools and colleges. But before we highlight key features of a creative lesson plan we need to examine what is meant by the term 'creative lesson'.

A creative lesson

A creative lesson is one which is designed or structured in a way that connects learning to real-life situations. It means the lesson aims and objectives, in addition to meeting assessment requirements, should demonstrate how the topic of the lesson relates or applies to the world outside the classroom (Ogunleye 2000). A creative lesson should also enable 'students to take the initiative for their own self-development and acquire the skills, understanding and flexibility to handle new situations with confidence' (FEU 1987: 6). According to FE teachers interviewed in an earlier work (Ogunleye 2002), the focus of a creative lesson will be students' involvement in class activities and how they are engaged in a lesson. In these teachers' views, a creative lesson should enable learners to gain insights into the issues they need to explore and should encourage learners to communicate these insights. In general, a creative lesson should be multifaceted and all-encompassing.

FE teachers in Ogunleye (2002: 187) gave a number of examples of a creative lesson that they said informed their lesson plans:

A creative lesson to me would be one where students are allowed to think for themselves, where students' prior knowledge somehow is assessed, where students interact together, where they produce their own work, their own thoughts, where it is validated and accepted and it is cherished, where students have some control over the learning experience, so that it is not a one-way, but a two-way process.

(teacher of health and social care, sixth-form college)

A creative lesson should also provide opportunity for group work:

I think a good mixed lesson is where you've got some sort of things like imparting of information, subject learning; a lot of questioning going on, a lot of activities. If you get the right balance in the classroom then the students will automatically respond to it.

(teacher of GNVQ leisure and tourism, FE college)

For a group of teachers in vocational courses and one in academic courses, a creative lesson should emphasize the application of knowledge – but students should first be provided with prerequisite (basic) skills, knowledge and information that should enable them to work independently or in a group:

I suppose where students have the opportunity to apply theory and knowledge to a situation and the opportunity to apply feedback and discuss
their points of view on the theory.

(teacher of GNVQ business, FE college)

Where it is appropriate, a creative lesson should contextualize
learning, where classroom learning draws on students' own experience and interests:

In the context of business studies, I think it is to try and draw on student
experience and to try to get them to think about what is being got across to
them in the classroom and relate it to their experience and now they can
see the relationship between the two.

(teacher of AVCE business, FE college)

A teacher cited the opportunity for 'simulation' as an important
criterion for a creative lesson:

Do you use examples by bringing in real-life situations? If you have boring
things like filing, how do you stimulate students to become interested in
filing (a requirement in the NVQ 2 administration course specification)?
You have to have lots of filing cabinets in the classroom and stimulate
them to be able to understand it and to enjoy doing it.

(teacher of NVQ administration, SF college)

More generally, a creative lesson will promote high student
input and less teaching structure; it will be interactive, cognitively
challenging, thought-provoking, developmental and engaging:

I don't think it matters what the students are engaged in, as long as they
are fully engaged.

(teacher of A level sociology, SF college)

Key features of a creative lesson plan

In a creative lesson plan, 'teacher activity' and 'student activity' will:

- provide opportunities for students to think by asking open-
  ended questions such as 'how might . . .' which draw on their
  experiences and interests;
- provide opportunities for students to interact together by
  embedding short, group tasks in lesson plans in order to check
  student understanding of what is been taught;

- enable students, depending on their age group, to have appropriate control over their learning experience (a piecemeal approach to giving learning responsibility and control should be initially tried out for 14–16 year olds especially in a mixed group of 14–19 – given that teaching styles in school tend to be teacher-centred);
- strike a balance between imparting knowledge, subject learning and questioning;
- identify beforehand relevant examples that draw on real-life situations to which students may relate.

Softly does it with your lesson planning

Having read this far, you may be tempted to conclude that fostering creativity in teaching and learning requires an elaborate lesson plan. Far from it. Creativity by nature is highly unpredictable; it remains what Cropley (2001) described as a psychological constellation. In teaching for creativity some writers argue that you need not be too specific in your lesson plan; some also argued that you need not have a lesson plan at all. If you live in the real world of further education that is subject to external impositions such as funding, inspections or quality assurance, you will agree that not having a lesson plan in the name of teaching for creativity (when emergent learning is not the objective) may land you in trouble with your line manager. What must be emphasized is that, whichever way you prepare your lesson plan, it should be flexible enough to focus your mind on what you set out to achieve in your lesson. As Sale (2004: 11) notes, part of your role as a teacher is to be creative 'in the flow of dialogues during the lesson'.

Teaching materials

I cannot emphasize this point enough: good lesson preparation aids lesson delivery by making it clearer and 'structural'. Teaching and learning materials are integral to lesson delivery. How beforehand you think through, find out, organize and prepare materials to use is key to effective delivery of lessons.

Preparing teaching material prior to use

Teachers may sometimes be spoilt for choice when choosing from a wide range of 'pre-packed' teaching and learning resources that are available in good bookshops and stationers. This makes it very tempting always to want to buy ready-made material rather than making your own. A disadvantage of using ready-made material is that it might not always be suitable for every student in your teaching group, especially if you have to teach a mixed group of 14–19 students. The younger learners may need help breaking down and digesting technical information, knowledge that the author of the material may have assumed that the students have. If you have to produce or make your own learning material such as handouts, be clear in your mind about what information should go into it and how you want the students to use this in addition to other 'who', 'what', 'where', 'when' and 'how' questions that you need to address (see Minton 2005).

Thinking through materials to use
To think through is to build a picture of the kinds of materials that might aid student learning in lessons; it is to picture how to arrange, organize and use teaching and learning materials to achieve the sole aim of enhancing student learning. Teaching and learning materials will cover everything from the overhead projector to student handouts. Ask yourself whether you really need to use OHP for the lesson you are preparing to teach or whether a detailed student handout is more suitable for the students. The latter point is particularly important. If you often end up collecting most of your lesson handouts because students leave them behind after class, then you need to ask yourself why you should continue to expend time and resources on 'detailed' handouts that only a few students bother to read. When introducing a topic for the first time, a better approach might be to produce *informational* handouts that nurse the students, especially the younger ones, into appreciating the need to find out more about the subject.

Thinking through beforehand materials to use in lessons will benefit both the student and the teacher. For the student, it will mean *using* handouts that provide *new* information rather than a duplication of what is available in the textbooks; for the teacher, it will mean saving time and energy by preparing teaching and learning materials that truly *aid* student learning.

Finding out and selecting teaching aids prior to use

It can be argued that finding out and selecting beforehand teaching aids to use in lessons should present little difficulty. The main challenge, however, is finding out and selecting the *right* teaching aids *appropriate* for the planned lesson. The *right teaching* aids will 'fit the purpose', meaning they will be suitable in lessons as intended in the plan; appropriate teaching aids will be relevant to the students' group. No teachers would want them to be above the heads of the students in the lesson – you should ensure that the teaching and learning aids are suitable. If you have to use the overhead projector, flip chart, interactive whiteboard or any other teaching aid, use it in the right context and for the right reasons – the overriding criterion for choosing aids for teaching and learning should be about enhancing student learning. You may have overheard colleagues in the staff rooms saying they used the OHP because they found it convenient. 'Lecturer convenience' should not be the main reason for using teaching aids! Teaching aids should be used because they enhance student learning. As a lecturer, you must get used to sacrificing your own personal convenience for the needs of your students.

Conclusion

In closing this chapter I would like to challenge you with this thought. As you prepare for each and every lesson, ask yourself this question: 'How do I turn every lesson into an exciting classroom experience for the students?' The next chapter will show you some techniques that you can use to make your teaching effective and to warm students to your teaching.

4 Effective teaching of the 14–16 group

Introduction

This chapter begins by highlighting key attributes of successful teachers of 14–16 year olds as a basis for developing effective teaching styles and techniques. It discusses a range of teaching techniques drawn from my work and that of others on 14–16 provision that can be adapted or used in a range of teaching situations. Among the suggested techniques are creative lesson introduction, good teacher questioning skills and variable teaching styles.

Keys to effective teaching of 14–16 year olds

There are four attributes that I found in highly successful teachers of 14–16 year olds which might have helped their teaching. The first is that they went out of their way to help students manage the transition from school to college. What your 14–16 group certainly does not want is academic discontinuity – when there is little or no linkage between students' learning experiences in school and college. If you are going to be teaching students from the same school, find out who their head of year is and meet with this person or chat over the phone to find out what the students already know about the subject.

The second attribute I found is that highly successful teachers made students *see the point* of coming to college for vocational learning. 14–16 year olds come to college full of expectations to learn in a new, bigger environment as well as to experience different approaches to teaching and learning. They expect to engage in learning in new, applied ways and they expect to connect to their individual vocational subjects. They expect teaching and learning methods to be interactive and practical, connecting students to the world around them. This is what vocational education is all about and that is what highly successful teachers of 14–16 year olds strive to give.

The third attribute is that highly successful teachers made it a duty to meet with students informally prior to their first lesson. This meeting could take place 10–15 minutes before the first lesson or a day before. Meeting students informally before their first lesson will help you to develop a rapport that will form the basis of your relationship with the students. Use this meeting to talk about your expectations of the students and what they can achieve on the course once they put their minds to it. Use this meeting to give the students a snapshot of the topics you intend to cover in the next few weeks and demonstrate how these topics build on or develop their existing knowledge. Use this meeting to explain the differences in teaching and learning methods used in school and college. Throughout this meeting, encourage the students to ask questions about your expectations on the course or about teaching and learning in college and answer their questions as best as you can.

The fourth attribute – and probably the most important – that I found in highly successful teachers is that they liked to take the creative challenge. As a creative teacher, you will reflect on your teaching techniques and you will constantly seek a new, better way to deliver your lessons. Your students will have a clear idea of the topic you intend to teach in the next lesson, but will have no idea about *how* you will deliver it. It is not that you consciously like to keep students guessing about your teaching styles – far from it; they just cannot characterize your teaching by any particular styles. By 'breathing' new life into both familiar and unfamiliar topics, week after week, you will get students to connect to the subject and therefore to turn up regularly for lessons. The question is, are you ready to take the creative challenge? Before I show you some of the creative techniques that you can apply or adapt to your teaching situations, I need to examine the context for creativity in teaching and learning in 14–16 education so that you rest assured that it is not just a desirable thing to be a creative teacher; it is also what the government desires for you! Not to put too fine a point on it, you need to be creative to be an effective teacher.

The context for creativity in teaching and learning in 14–16 education

In 1998, the government showed an interest in creativity when it established the National Advisory Committee on Creative and Cultural Education (NACCCE), chaired by Professor Ken Robinson, formerly of Warwick University. NACCCE was asked to examine how creativity can be encouraged, enhanced and supported in the development of young people and the role of the education system in preparing them for the social, economic and cultural demands of the new century. NACCCE submitted its report in 1999, which included a wide range of recommendations. The four-part report (DfEE 1999) addressed issues such as the difficulty of defining creativity, development of creativity in the curriculum, creativity and teaching and learning, and schools' links with outside organizations and agencies.

NACCCE's definition of creativity is premised upon four characteristics of creative processes: imagination, purpose, originality and value. Creativity is defined as 'imaginative activity fashioned so as to produce outcomes that are both original and of value' (DfEE 1999: 29). The report explored these processes and underlined the importance of practical application of knowledge, in all fields, as central to developing young learners' creative abilities. It proposed that education provide opportunities for young learners to express their ideas, values, feelings and imagination.

The report identified two themes that NACCCE believed would have implications for arrangements and delivery of the curriculum. They are the need to underpin the concept of creativity with knowledge, and to give learners the freedom and confidence to experiment (p. 38). It acknowledged that unrestrained, unfocused or non-goal specific creativity can be counterproductive and might be of little value. A brief review preceded the NACCCE assertion that the National Curriculum has not served the cause of creative education. Factors such as the policy instability that has characterized curriculum organization and structure in schools, and high levels of pre-scription on schools have impeded creativity in the school curriculum. The report proposed that official policy state-ments and government rationale for the compulsory education curriculum must make explicit reference to the importance of creativity in teaching and learning. It urged governments at both local and national levels to effect a reduction in current levels of external prescription on schools and to allow schools greater freedom and flexibility in the arrangements and deli-very of a 'broad and balanced' curriculum. It proposed that creativity be promoted in all areas of the curriculum and across subject disciplines.

The report identified the need for creativity in teaching and learning, by making a link between creative teaching and creative learning; it said both are complementary and not mutually exclusive. It rejected the debate about the choice between traditional teaching methods and progressive teaching methods, arguing instead that a balance be struck to enable the best of the two methods to be combined. There is clearly the need for teaching strategies to emphasize content and skills, as well as the need for teaching methods to provide opportunity for learners to enquire, experiment, question and express thoughts and ideas.

The report offers a two-pronged concept to nurture cre-ativity in teaching and learning: teaching creatively and teach-ing for creativity. In teaching creatively, the teacher's role is to encourage young people's autonomy and belief in their own creative ability; another role is to help discover or identify their creative strengths and abilities; and help them to develop and foster their creativity by developing ordinary ability and skills; 'common' capacities and sensitivities; and understand-ing of creative processes. A teacher's role in teaching for cre-ativity includes providing an enabling environment in which learners can feel the confidence to make mistakes, to take risks and to work; encouraging freedom, self-expression of ideas, thoughts and values; stimulating curiosity and imagination and originality through the free play of ideas.

Top tips for effective teaching of 14–16 year olds

Now that you know something of the context for creativity in teaching and learning in 14–16 education, I present in the following paragraphs a summary of creative teaching techniques derived from our work and others' on 14–16 provision in further education. Applying or adapting these techniques will help you to become an effective teacher of 14–16 year olds, rest assured.

Use creative lesson introductions

Most good restaurants will offer you a 'starter' while you are waiting for the main course. A starter is designed to whet your appetite for the main course. As teachers, we often do not attach as great importance to attention-getting lesson starters as we should. What we have sometimes passed off as lesson starters, quite frankly, are no more than a summary of the last lesson or an introduction to the next. Your lesson starter should serve a dual purpose: to introduce the lesson and at the same time whet the students' appetite for it. One idea of a lesson starter in a business studies class where students are examining marketing and sales strategies might be to bring two identical sets of chocolate bars to class and get students to explain why one set costs twice as much as the other. You might also use a short conversation as a lesson starter. In a food technology class in which students are looking at food poisoning, you might take a controversial line which says 'Stores should be allowed to sell processed foods up to a day after their sell-by date', and then ask students to argue for or against. In a child-care and development class in which students are looking at child abuse, a five-minute video clip about how adults might abuse children in their care can be shown at the start of lesson and you could ask students to discuss the scenario. You can use any starter; the only criterion is that it must totally capture students' interest. Using starters gives you the flexibility to begin your lesson right away without having to wait for the whole group to arrive. When students come in to lesson, they know that there is always an activity or a discussion they can join in.

Vary the pace of your lesson

Your awareness of the speed of your lesson delivery is key to becoming an effective teacher. Think of the lesson pace as the 'speed' of the lesson in a period. This will include how long you intend to spend on 'teacher activity' such as presentation and questioning; on 'student activity' such as group work, individual work, questioning, students' practice and application of newly taught skills and knowledge. In secondary schools, a lesson period varies between 50 minutes and one hour; in further education colleges, a lesson period might take between one and a half to three hours. There is, therefore, no rule of thumb for determining the pace at which teachers should deliver lessons; the key determinants are the students' group, the topic of presentation and the teaching techniques. However, the overriding consideration should be your students' needs and abilities and it is important to ensure that the pace of your lesson is appropriate to the student group. Some students work fast and some work a little more slowly. For example, you will slow the pace when introducing new topics and you will increase the pace when reviewing topics – in doing this, you are making class activities challenging for the high-ability students and do-able for the average ability students. Remember also that Key Stage 4 students are more likely to switch off after a more than one-hour lesson (Ogunleye and McNay 2005); it is therefore important to ensure that they are engaged in classroom activities at least 85 to 90 per cent of lesson time. By appropriately pacing your lessons, you will cover everything you set out to do in the lesson plan.

Challenge your students

If students do not find your first few lessons challenging enough, they will soon label it 'boring' and it will be a hard job getting them to tune in again in subsequent ones. You certainly do not want students to attend your lessons for the wrong reason – because they are mandated to do so. You want them to turn up for lessons because they are learning something and enjoying the subject. You can challenge students on three fronts – in the way you present lessons, the way you set class work and the way you set homework – by asking questions or setting them activities that arouse interest for the subject and the learning process.

Develop good questioning skills

Good questioning skills are characteristics of effective teaching, which can help to stimulate students' creative thinking. Questioning activity is an excellent way to build, nurture and sustain students' enquiring minds. Questioning is 'a valuable part of the teaching–learning process because it enables participants, teachers and students, to establish what is already known, to use and extend this knowledge and then to develop new ideas' (Painter 1996). Knowing how and when to ask questions may not come naturally to you, but it is important to develop the skill. An earlier work by the author found that FE students and lecturers seldom ask questions in lessons (Ogunleye 2002). Someone has to 'break the ice' and that person has to be you. If you want to become effective in your teaching, you need to ask questions frequently in lessons, especially during the presentation bit of the 'teacher activity'. Ask questions according to the particular demands of the topic you are teaching; ask open-ended or divergent questions if you desire to develop student enquiry and creative thinking. Divergent questions will require no single answers; they are particularly useful when you want to seek clarification from students – an example is 'what do you mean by that?' They are also useful when you want students to shed light on, or to justify, their answers. You can also use questioning to challenge or motivate students to learn, to reinforce teaching, to check on the students' progress and to manage and control classroom.

Relate learning to real world
'Connecting learning to the real world produces excellence', says Dale Parnell, a founding father of the American community college system (Parnell 1999). To relate learning to its real-world context is to use community and workplace problems to underpin your teaching. If you are teaching forms of business ownership to applied business studies students, use a local 'corner shop' with which students are familiar. Ask students to highlight key characteristics of the shop and use their answers as a context for teaching about sole traders. If you are teaching vehicle roadworthiness and safety in a motor vehicle class, ask students to visit an MOT garage beforehand or to ask a vehicle-owning adult why vehicles need to have an MOT test and then use their feedback as a basis for your teaching. Remember that to motivate students to learn and sustain their interest in the subject, you must get them actively involved in lessons. Highly successful teachers try to make

students see the point of turning up for lessons by connecting learning to the world around their students. You should emulate them.

Use humour to a good effect

Young learners told me they like lecturers who 'use jokes' in lessons. I certainly do not encourage you to take on a comic character in lessons, but a tinge of rib-tickling jokes used sparingly or unconsciously in lessons can aid student–teacher interaction and build rapport. To use humour to a good effect, you need to ensure that the joke relates to the topic that is being taught. You should never use humour to embarrass students or to make sarcastic remarks about them.

Vary teaching styles

Make it a habit to vary your teaching styles in *every* lesson. Use teacher exposition or whole-class teaching, for example if you are introducing a new topic. Get students to work individually and go round the class to offer one-to-one support, for example if they need to develop particular technical skills; encourage small-team discussion where you require divergent answers to particular questions or class tasks.

Minimize the use of textbook

Teachers in the school sector tend to distribute textbooks to students at the start of lessons, thereby encouraging over-reliance on them. Aside from the fact that in FE you are unlikely to have enough textbooks to go round, you should minimize the use of textbooks in lessons; instead, create better, alternative resources, such as worksheets and information handouts.

Be sensitive to students' needs

Key Stage 4 students are quite aware of their personalities and can be sensitive to their environment. Remember that in the 14–16 age group, students can have many worries, not the least worries about their physical appearance and social popularity. Be sensitive to their individual and collective needs and appreciate them. Respect and value their opinions and have high expectations of them.

Keep to time

Keep to time and manage it well during lessons. If you ask students to attempt class activities, say precisely in how many minutes you want them to complete the activities – let your 7 minutes be that – 7 minutes. Think about other users of the classroom too: don't keep colleagues and other student groups hanging around waiting for you to finish your class.

Manage behaviours

Many FE teachers told us they can do without classroom management. But let's face it, we live in the real world and it is inevitable that you will have to deal with behaviour problems in your lessons. Highly successful teachers manage students' behaviours by being firm, but friendly, to get their attention. They do not shout and get angry with students, neither do they have a template response to every behaviour situation in their lessons. They are mindful about how they challenge students who ask each other intermittent questions about the topic they were teaching. They knew that students might have been doing so because they were not able to follow the presentation. You can remedy a situation such as this by encouraging students to direct their questions to you rather than engaging in side-discussions. However, there are behaviours that you may want to challenge, especially if they are quite disruptive – such as throwing paper, moving around without reason or noisily blowing gum bubbles during lessons. You might not have to experience any of these behaviours if you and the students have had some agreement at the start of the course on what constitutes disruptive behaviour in lessons.

Prepare students for the next lesson

Whet the appetite of the students for their next lesson. Use the closing section of today's lesson to introduce the students to new vocabulary or technical information that they might need to learn for the next lesson; talk them through it, explain its relevance and demonstrate how the topic relates to a real-life situation (Ogunleye 2002). If you think the students need to do some background reading beforehand, encourage them to do so. One way to encourage 14–16 year olds to read up on a particularly difficult topic beforehand is to form them into mixed teams of abilities and get every student in the team to answer different questions on their team's findings. Notice that I use the word *team* and not group.

Conclusion

As I close this chapter, I should remind you of the core attributes of successful teachers of 14–16 year olds from my observations: they helped students to make the transition from school to college; they made students see the point of coming to college for vocational learning; they made it a duty to meet with students prior to their first lesson; and, most importantly, they liked to take the creative challenge. I would encourage you to adopt these attributes and apply the accompanying techniques to your teaching situations. Over time you will know if you have been an effective teacher: this is when students demonstrate an improved understanding of the subject as they become more confident; when students participate more in lessons, by asking probing questions and responding to challenging questions; and when students raise the quality of their work as evidenced by higher grades in coursework or mock assessments. Good evidence will also include student performance in external assessments or examinations such as GCSE.

In the next chapter, I show you how you can equally become an effective teacher of 16–19 year olds.

5 Effective teaching of the 16–19 group

Introduction

Methods used in teaching 14–16 year olds can also be applied or adapted for use in teaching 16–19 year olds, as well as in teaching students aged 19 and over. At the risk of repetition, the aim of this chapter is to expand on some of the teaching techniques described in chapter 4, but with specific reference to the 16–19 age group.

Housekeeping matters

Appreciate the teaching demands of 16–19 year olds

As a trained FE teacher you should naturally feel at home teaching 16–19 year olds, but work by Allan and Gartside (1989) suggests that both experienced and new teachers have difficulty in certain areas of their teaching. These 'difficult' areas include facing the class for the first time, coping with mixed-ability students and with class discipline. What was interesting about Allan and Gartside's findings were the differences in view expressed by the two categories of the lecturers interviewed. For example, 54 per cent of the experienced lecturers perceived facing a class for the first time as a teaching difficulty, compared with 28 per cent of the new lecturers. 51 per cent of the experienced lecturers considered coping with mixed-ability groups a teaching difficulty, compared with 22 per cent of the new lecturers. 34 per cent of the experienced lecturers considered coping with class discipline a teaching difficulty, compared with 19 per cent of the new lecturers. According to the authors, the differences in view were 'possibly a cause for concern, particularly where lecturers are failing to apprehend the importance of the skills of teaching' (Allan and Gartside 1989: 3).

These findings did not necessarily mean that the new lecturers were better at handling certain teaching difficulties than were their more experienced colleagues; it is possible that the new lecturers might have been overconfident, while their more experienced colleagues might have been realistic; other reasons are also possible. What is important to note is that no two students' groups are identical in terms of ability, prior knowledge and learning attributes. Each student cohort will present you with its own, unique set of challenges to which you will have to respond.

Help students to settle in

What makes teaching 16–19 year olds in their first month/term in college a little challenging, as some teachers in Allan and Gartside's survey found, is that there are few transition arrangements between Years 11 and 12 that enable students to have an appreciation of the learning environment in FE. The 16 year olds, in their first month in FE, are likely to behave as if they are still in school. You will do well to help them to settle into the new learning environment (helping students to settle in the college should not be seen as sole responsibility of the student services). Make it clear to students what your expectations are – for example, tell them you expect them to take responsibility for their own learning, to attend regularly and to be actively involved in lessons. Then explain to them how you might help them to meet these expectations.

Effective teaching of 16–19 year olds

The following paragraphs highlight some of the techniques used by teachers of 16–19 year olds in our survey (see Ogunleye 2002); they are best used to supplement the techniques discussed in chapter 4.

Good use of questioning

Questioning is at the heart of teaching, but a good use of questioning techniques is more than asking questions frequently in lessons. As a teacher, you need to ask yourself whether the questions you ask in the classroom make cognitive demands on your students (Chandhari 1975). Asking probing or cognitively demanding questions is essential to developing student thinking skills. As already mentioned in chapter 4, asking 'what would happen if . . .' questions will help develop your students' divergent thinking skills. Use a mixture of open-ended and closed questions to get your students actively involved in the classroom. A teacher of the 16–19 group we observed used puzzles and paradoxes, in the form of questions, to tease out responses from his students. The technique worked – it encouraged the students to think through before answering the teacher's questions. Identify what works best for your students. Effective use of questioning also helps teachers to ascertain students' prior knowledge and understanding of particular topics under discussion (Curzon 1997).

Pre-teach subject vocabulary terms

Too often as teachers we try to load students with new learning or material before they master the basics of the subject or the topic we teach. Students will do well in your subject if you develop their understanding of the basics of the subject or the subject vocabulary terms. Pre-teach the subject basics or the vocabulary terms. By the subject 'basics' or 'vocabulary terms' I mean teaching the students the rudiments of the subject, breaking down technical terms and information. Once the students understand the basics, give them self-directed project work to apply their knowledge. The projects on vocational engineering courses might include researching items for designing basic and specialist tools or improving basic tools.

Connect learning to the real world

As already mentioned in the previous chapter, you can aid student knowledge application and knowledge transformation by putting students' prior knowledge into context or by relating learning to real-life situations. One way to do this is to provide opportunities for students to 'simulate' a real-life situation or problem in the classroom. Take the teaching of NVQ 2 administration, for example. One way to teach topics such as filing is to have a reasonable amount of strategically placed filing cabinets in the classroom and use the setting as a basis to teach the topic. This approach will help you to keep your lesson as close to what is expected in a real-life business office as possible.

Raise confidence

Raising student confidence is key to engaging 16–19 year olds in learning. Help your students to develop self-confidence in your class. Start with student activities. In setting written activities, ask relatively easy questions at the beginning and ask more challenging questions as the students progress in the activities. Another way to raise your students' self-confidence in the classroom is by helping them to develop independence of thought and learning, by allowing them to express themselves in classroom discussion, especially where the questions for discussion do not require yes or no answers.

Frequent feedback

Be honest, how long do you take to provide feedback to students on their work? If you do not provide frequent, early feedback to your students you are not helping them to learn as much as they should and as fast as they should. When you give students tasks to do in lesson, go round the class and mark as many students' answers as possible. Students need to know how they are doing now and then. If you must collect their work to mark outside lessons because of time constraints, ensure that students receive feedback on their work as soon as you can possibly turn it around. A delayed feedback sometimes demotivates students; it could prompt them to ask 'what is the point . . .' questions. When your students cannot see the point in doing your assignment, you will almost certainly lose them to attrition.

Vary teaching styles

Vary your teaching styles. Provide opportunities for group work as well as encourage students to work individually in situations where you want to develop individual application of knowledge. Experiment with problem-solving teaching styles. Problem-solving is the ability to generate new ways to attain a goal, the ability to adapt prior learning to new situations and the ability to acquire a new pattern of responses (Jones 1972). It is a characteristic of creative thinking, which aims to find solutions to problems. The steps in techniques of problem-solving include: describing the situation, fact finding, stating the problem, searching for a solution, implementing the solution, evaluating the implemented solution and proposing modification or improvement of the solution (Labelle 1974). Key to facilitating problem-solving skills in the classroom is breaking students' previous patterns of thinking (Cackowski 1969), as well as developing their cognitive skills. You can also experiment with reading assignments. Students can be encouraged to learn the history of the subject to facilitate 'bonds' between the students and the subject.

Make your lesson a haven of activities

It was suggested in the last chapter that a significant part of your lesson should be activity-based. A good lesson should be a beehive of learning activities – 85 to 90 per cent of your lesson time should be used for classroom activities that may consist of student presentation, question and answer, written or oral discussions, etc. If you are using discussion, ensure that the context is clearly set out or the problem is clearly identified; ensure that the learning resources such as worksheets and (information) handouts are available and in sufficient quantity; and ensure that different groups are engaged in different activities.

Embed ICT in your lessons

Make it a habit to use information and communication technology (ICT) in your teaching as regularly and as appropriately as possible. Computer graphics, animation and computer simulation may be used, for example, to teach students whose cognitive disposition might not favour learning in traditional classroom settings. Older, non–ICT-based subject teachers are said to be less enthusiastic about using IT in their teaching. If you are one of those teachers, I would encourage you to reflect critically about your teaching practice (see chapter 8 for helpful hints on continuing personal development). Given the prevalence of ICT in most course specifications, it is hard to see how any teacher can keep it out of their teaching.

Conclusion

This chapter has attempted to expand on a selected number of techniques from among those discussed in chapter 4. Techniques such as questioning, variable teaching styles and the use of ICT are key to effective teaching of 16–19 year olds. In examining these techniques, this chapter has reinforced a central theme of this book – that you can sustain students' interest in lessons through effective teaching methods and practices. You can sustain students' interest in your subject when you make subject matter and the mode of teaching interesting, when you encourage whole-class involvement and participation while, simultaneously, making academic tasks cognitively challenging, as writers such as Stevenson (1990) have argued. Turn now to the next chapter for ideas on how to teach a mixed group of 14–19 year olds.

6 Effective teaching of the 14–19 mixed-age group

Introduction

This chapter examines a somewhat challenging aspect of FE teachers' work – teaching a mixed class of 14–19 year olds. It points out a situation in which a lecturer might be required to teach a mixed-age lesson and highlights key techniques that can be used or applied in a variety of teaching situations. The techniques highlighted are drawn from the author's work with 14–19 year olds in further education.

Prepare to teach a mixed-age group

A common question that is often asked in this era of school–college partnerships is how best to cater for the needs of the thousands of pupils who attend vocational classes in further education colleges every week. Should colleges integrate the pupils into the regular 16–19 groups or should the pupils be provided with discrete classes? Or should colleges run parallel 'infill' and discrete classes? For many colleges, however, the state of their finances and other issues such as curriculum arrangements, timetabling and room availability are the key factors in deciding how courses for 14–16 year olds are organized. What I found from my work in FE is that lecturers are increasingly being asked to teach mixed-age classes; this is where 14–16 year olds are *infilled* or put in the same class as older students; the older group may be doing level 2 or GCSE equivalent qualifications. Teaching across the age divide is both fun and challenging. It is challenging because it requires a lot of planning and preparation as well as your ability as a lecturer to deliver lessons at different levels and paces to meet the needs of every student in the class. The challenge of meeting the needs of every student in a mixed-age class is aptly summarized by this 17 year old:

What I like is different [teaching] techniques, which will make it [the lesson] more interesting. When the teacher asks me a question, to make sure that I understand it; to use examples, to make it interesting; to test our understanding. To use different techniques.

The following paragraphs highlight some of the techniques you can use to teach a mixed-age class.

Welcome students with a smile

Key Stage 4 students have their own way of doing things. We observed that they would turn up for lessons almost at the same time or in small groups and they would take a few minutes or longer to settle into the 'learning mood'. Older students would stroll into the classroom one after the other or come in triads. Make eye contact with students as they come into the class and welcome them with an assuring beam. When students come late to lesson, challenge them with concern, but avoid confrontation. Remind them of the rule they signed up to at the start of term (if this was the case) that they will endeavour to come to lesson on time. I know from my work with 14–19 year olds that they do not like being told off; they prefer teachers to speak to them politely or to challenge them with concern. As one 15 year old student put it:

Teachers should be more influential, to care about the students. I know I come late sometimes, but I want to feel that teachers do care about why I come late. To show a bit of compassion, I think.

(Ogunleye and McNay 2005: 25)

As students come into the class, don't keep the 'early birds' waiting for the rest of the group; use lesson starters discussed in chapter 4 to arouse and sustain students' interest while you wait for others to arrive.

Use your voice effectively

You need good voice projection skills to teach a mixed class effectively. Project your voice effectively by talking at students head up if you are standing in front facing the class. Get the tonal balance of your voice right – it should not be too loud, nor should it be too low. Try not to stand in the same spot for too long when you teach. A teacher I observed literally stood still in a corner to the right of the students; he had to talk from the top of his voice so that he could be heard by everyone in the room. Be careful about the effect of talking too loud on your voice box. Try this method: depending on the size and layout of the classroom, try to move around as you speak and ask questions intermittently to check students' knowledge. Effective use of your voice will increase your confidence in your ability to communicate.

Avoid asking students to copy notes from the whiteboard

You may use the whiteboard or overhead projector to outline the lesson aims and objectives, but avoid asking students to copy long notes from the whiteboard or overhead projector even if it is something that your 14–16 year olds have been used to in school. This practice may not be suitable for your 16–19 group. One 18 year old student told me that copying notes from the board did not help her to learn; another student said he found it boring. Another student remarked:

As you can see [in your classroom observation], the lesson was boring. All you do is copying things from the OHP. It turns you off.

Instead, use information handouts or sheets for the mixed group, but ensure that the handout is simplified for the 14–16 group, yet detailed enough for the 16–19 group.

Develop group cohesiveness

14–16 year olds are self-conscious; they can be sensitive as to how they relate to others and can also be sensitive as to how others perceive them, as demonstrated in the following comments by a 15 year old infill student:

I suppose it's [having my Key Stage 4 lessons in college is] OK. They put us with older students. Sometime they [older students] gave us a funny look.

(Ogunleye and McNay 2005: 35)

Your students may not want to accept each other, partly because they lack social skills to interact or work together; it is also possible that they have had no time to bond as a team. It is important to facilitate a sense of team spirit or togetherness across the age divide. Your role as a teacher therefore is to foster an atmosphere of cooperation in the classroom; this will help to avoid the sort of situation described above by the 15 year old. One way to develop group cohesiveness is to organize a pre-lesson session where the whole group is made to engage in practical discussions. Use well-thought-out, practical questions which allow students to 'own' the discussions; for instance, you may ask questions that require students to use their personal experiences as a basis for their answers. Another way to develop a spirit of cooperation across the age groups is to divide up the class for lesson activities, presentations or investigative activities. Assign students into groups using *unusual* interests or hobbies. For example, ask students who liked to ride camels as birthday treats to join an assigned group. Repeat the process using differing interests or hobbies until you get everyone assigned to a group. As you assign students to groups, aim for an equal balance of younger and older students. Putting the students into mixed groups will encourage them to work with those other students with whom they do not normally interact. If you teach a very small class, limit the number of students per group to two – one younger and one older – and when it is time for feedback to the class, let each student give the other's response. This technique of getting each person to give the response of the other person in the group will encourage students to listen and cooperate with each other.

Encourage students to take responsibility for their own learning

Your 14–16 year old students are used to being led by the teacher and might not be particularly keen to take responsibility for their learning. In school, it is common for students to be given workbooks or textbooks from which to work; it is common to have students' work checked or marked during lessons; it is also common for school teachers to come to lessons with 'spare' pens and writing pads. This last practice is said to be viewed in FE as 'student pampering', but it is a simple case of accepting 14–16 year olds as they are. And if that means bringing enough 'spare' pencils, pens and writing pads to lessons to help them to learn, it's worth it. Ensure that you have enough workbooks or textbooks to go round

– 14–16 year olds in FE told me they do not like to share books! As the students adjust to their new environment and grapple with new concepts of learning, do everything possible to help them to learn. You will do well to demonstrate why the students should look forward to your next lesson. Your 16–19 year olds should be clear about what you expect from them, which will include an acceptance that they take responsibility for their own learning. Remind them what those expectations are if you need to; reinforce those expectations if you have to. Although you do not expect to provide older students with pens and writing pads, you will do well to bring 'spares' for a handful of them. Do everything possible to help everyone in the class to learn.

Sustain students' interest

In FE, the period of a lesson varies from one and a half to two hours, or even three hours. Your 16–19 group may have got used to a longer lesson period, but this may be new to your 14–16 group. What I found in my work in FE is that lecturers quite often found it challenging to sustain Key Stage 4 students' interest when lessons go over 50 minutes or one hour, which is an average lesson period in secondary schools. If you have a double-lesson period, ensure that you pack the lesson with a variety of activities for each of the student groups. This means using variable teaching methods; depending on your subject, whole-class teaching, group teaching and one-to-one teaching can all be integrated and used in a double-period session. If you use whole-class teaching, use questioning fairly frequently to check or reinforce students' learning. When delivering whole-class teaching, help your students to learn by using simple words and explain technical terms very clearly – remember that your 16–19 group may be more familiar with the subject's technical terms than is your 14–16 group.

You can pre-teach the subject's vocabulary terms or provide a breakdown of the technical terms in a handout written mainly for the 14–16 group: this should also benefit the 16–19 group. If you use group teaching, use practical or hands-on activities to engage students; the use of hands-on activities is particularly suitable in vocational lessons. You can also vary class activities within a particular age group by not giving every student the same tasks to do at the same time. This is how a teacher of English in 14–18 provision (high school) I observed during a study in the United States (Ogunleye 2003) said she attempts to differentiate class or homework activities to suit individual student groups:

We don't require that all students are doing the same thing – they all have different projects. In every kind of assignment that we create we try to find different ways to satisfy that assignment.

There are other things you can do to sustain students' interest in mixed-age lessons. It might be useful to use colour markers to write key points or technical terms on the whiteboard. The use of colour markers along with the 'traditional' black colour markers is said to 'catch' the attention of younger learners or 'fascinate' older learners. Try also to use different learning aids in every lesson: you can use pictorial representations, symbols, objects, diagrams, etc. and embed some of these in your lessons. Another way to sustain students' interest in lesson is to personalize class activities. Ask classroom questions or set homework tasks in a way that allows every student to express themselves. Weaker students on vocational courses, for example, said they learn better when class or homework activities encouraged them to reflect their thoughts or their (informed) opinions in their answers; or to graphically present their work as they deem fit. A teacher of vocational courses explains how he encourages students' self-expression in learning output (e.g. work presentation):

[By] letting students express things in the way they want or in the way they best do. Teaching Business Studies does involve theory and does involve number and I am quite happy for them to present the theory to me in any form they want – in the form of tables or bar charts – they can do that.

Relate teaching to the world around students

My work with Key Stage 4 students in FE shows that 14–16 year olds want to connect to their subjects; by 'connecting' they mean demonstrating a subject's real-life relevance or application. The use of real-life problems will help your students to interact with the real world. If you teach travel and tourism it is best to make use of real-life travel brochures or tourist information to contextualize your exposition or set the scene for class discussions or use as a basis for teaching in a question and answer session. A child-care and development teacher of 14–18 year olds I observed in the same American study explains how she tries to connect learning to the world around her students:

I think one thing that makes it [teaching] pretty easy is that the students here see children. They see the point of doing the lessons. If we are talking about strengthening finger muscles, etc., they can see how it relates to real life. Students are always kind of reminded that it is a real pre-school, it is not pretend, and it is just like [any other] workplace. So, it is connected and I think the students know it is connected.

A teacher of hotel and catering explains how she, too, relates her teaching to real-life situations:

It [teaching] all relates to material we use. I used a variety of booklets, meeting and convention planning booklets. I get every package from all the hotels I can possibly get and I do on a timely basis – any time we are doing a unit, more letters go out. If you open a convention booklet from Las Vegas, etc., you make it [the lesson] very real, better than if I were just to give them a piece of paper and say here is how they do it, it is not real. I got the entire whole room back there full of materials, newspapers, weekly magazines, etc.

In England, an FE lecturer explains how he tries to contextualize his teaching 'to make things a bit different from the norm and more appealing and exciting to students'. He added:

I teach the AVCE Business finance unit, which is usually quite a dry sub-ject. I would add a bit of realism into it, a bit of things that make students think.

Praise students regularly in lessons

A simple, time-tested way to motivate students to learn is to praise them regularly for their efforts! This may sound simple, but you would be surprised to know that lecturers hardly praise students in the classroom (see chapter 7). Many students like to take a step at a time – when answering teachers' questions or when attempting class or homework activities – and they want to be sure each step is 'right' before they take the next. They need help from you to raise their self-confidence to participate in lessons. So, let the students know they are making progress, praise the smallest positive step.

When you praise students each time they participate in class activities or answer your question, even if the answer was incorrect, you are helping them to develop confidence in their ability to engage in the classroom.

Adapt learning material to meet every student's needs

Although you may prefer to use standard textbooks such as the recommended subject-specific textbooks for your class, you should not assume that these books will meet the need of every student; there will be some students who will find it difficult to read and understand standard textbooks. You will do well to supplement textbooks with tailored handouts or worksheets to meet the needs of weaker students.

Provide clearer information to students about their coursework

14–19 year old students want clearer, unambiguous information about their coursework; students tend to give a higher priority, in terms of effort and time, to coursework than to class or homework activities, because coursework grades are often taken into account in final assessments. Listen to what this 15 year old has to say:

Our [college] teachers gave us work and they don't tell us it is coursework. They just give it to us to do. And when we do it we may not take it seriously. Then later on, they tell us that it is coursework and we have to go back and do it again.

If you put yourself in your students' position, you may understand why they want clearer information about any work that you ask them to do. When you give students coursework, include enough pointers on how to go about doing it; encourage them to show you their work in the draft form before they submit formally; your students will appreciate your commitment towards their studies.

Use homework effectively

Use homework to reinforce student learning. Ensure that worksheets and learning materials are differentiated with homework activities clearly marked for the 14–16 group. Set homework also for the 16–19 group to check and reinforce their learning. Ensure that you mark the students' work and give them timely feedback.

The students will form their own opinion about your professional-ism if you take too much time to mark their work and feed back to them. Next time, they may not be too keen to turn in their work on time.

Conclusion

This chapter has highlighted key techniques that can be used to teach effectively in a mixed-age class. Teaching a mixed-age class requires good preparation and planning (see chapter 3), as well as your ability as a lecturer to deliver lessons at different levels and paces across the age divide. In a mixed-age class, you can, among other things, use your voice effectively, develop group cohesiveness, relate teaching to the world around students and encourage them to take responsibility for their own learning. The next chapter pre-sents research findings on FE teachers' classroom behaviours and practices; these are keys to effective teaching of 14–19 year olds.

7 Keys to effective teaching of 14–19 students

Introduction

This chapter presents the results of a study of teaching and learning in further education. It provides insights into the students' perceptions of their own approaches to learning in the classroom as well as their perceptions of their classroom teachers' behaviours and practices. It also highlights findings from a series of classroom observations designed to cross-validate or corroborate the students' views on issues such as the teacher question ratio and motivation in the classroom.

Students' approaches to learning

You need a good understanding of students' classroom behaviours and practices in your striving for excellence in teaching; these behaviours and practices are defined, in this context, as features of classroom interaction, learning style, preference and disposition. The following paragraphs provide a snapshot of findings from a study conducted in four sixth-form and six general further education colleges. 555 students participated in this study, which explored, among other things, students' approaches to learning in the classroom, as well as teachers' classroom behaviours and practices (Ogunleye 2002).

Students' questions

The study found that 35 per cent of the students ask questions regularly in lessons; 65 per cent of the students occasionally or rarely ask questions in lessons. The message from these findings is that you should encourage your students to ask questions in lessons more frequently; it is a good way to get your students to participate fully in the classroom.

Students' self-confidence

The study found that 60 per cent of the students avoid answering their classroom teacher's questions for fear of getting the answer wrong; only 40 per cent or fewer students have the self-confidence to answer classroom teacher's questions without having to worry that their answer might be wrong. These results underlined the importance of helping all students to develop their self-confidence; you should not have a situation where over half of your class is held back from answering your questions because of their lack of self-confidence.

Group work

The study also found that 43 per cent of the students felt regularly inspired working in a group; 57 per cent of the students felt occasionally or rarely inspired working in group. If you have heard that teachers' encouragement of group work in class activities aids active learning or creative interaction, you should not let these results change that message. What these results mean is that you will do well to encourage students to work on their own as often as you encourage them to work in groups (note that a third of the students in the same study generally prefer to work on their own).

Learning approach and preference

The study also found that 63 per cent of the students generally preferred to work within 'tried and trusted' methods in class activities and assignments; 37 per cent of the students preferred to innovate or express themselves in their work. You can wean students from this 'play-safe' habit by being flexible in the way you set your assignments; for instance, let your assignments give students a chance to find solutions to problems as often as possible. Also, encourage students to use a variety of methods – charts, graphical representations, illustration – to present their work.

Teachers' classroom behaviours and practices

The students were also asked about their perceptions of their classroom teacher's behaviours and practices, defined in this context as features of interaction such as motivation, thinking, praise, teacher subject knowledge, teacher question ratio and reference to practical examples or real-life situations in the classroom.

53 per cent of the students in the study believed their classroom teacher motivated them regularly to learn the subject; 47 per cent of the students believed their classroom teacher rarely or occasionally motivated them to learn the subject. The study also found that teachers do not praise students regularly in lessons – for instance, less than a third (31 per cent) of the students said their classroom teacher praises them regularly whenever possible. But FE teachers may have got it right on a number of issues; they only need to build on those as they strive for excellence in teaching. For example, an overwhelming majority of the students – 89 per cent – believed their classroom teacher demonstrates subject knowledge all or most of the time in lesson. This is encouraging to know; it confirms the age-old students' perception of teachers as reservoirs of knowledge. Another positive finding is that students believed their classroom teacher regularly encourages them to take responsibility for their work. As already mentioned in the previous paragraph, it is important to remind your 16–19 group regularly of this responsibility while developing it gradually in your 14–16 group. Another positive finding is that most teachers are 'open' to students' views most of the time in lessons, according to 73 per cent of the students. You, too, can demonstrate openness in your teaching by asking your students, for example, how best they thought they might approach a particular classroom discussion or presentation. You will have a good base to develop rapport with your students in the classroom if they believe that you are open to their views in the classroom.

Student–teacher interaction

The study reported in the following paragraphs used classroom observation to complement the student questionnaire. This was designed to record teacher–student interaction as it occurs and to cross-validate or corroborate students' perceptions of teachers' classroom behaviours and practices as reported earlier in the results from questionnaires. The analytical methods of the classroom observation data sets draw on Flanders' (1970) investigation of classroom interaction in the schools' sector.

Teacher talk

Teacher talk across further education colleges accounts for 80 per cent of the lesson time while student talk, silence or 'non-event' accounts for 20 per cent. These results tell us that there were very few pauses or non-events in the flow of classroom communication in the lessons observed. Another feature of student–teacher inter-action analysed is the teacher response ratio, defined as 'an index which corresponds to the teacher's tendency to react to the ideas and feelings of the students' (Flanders 1970: 102). The teacher response ratio is 22 per cent, well below the 42 per cent 'average' suggested by Flanders. This means that across further education colleges teachers do not respond often to students' talk nor give them time to talk in the classroom. In other words, there is less interaction between teacher and students than was observed by Flanders in the average school classroom during the 1960s–1970s when he carried out his studies.

Teacher question ratio

Teacher question ratio (TQR) is calculated to assess the teacher's 'tendency to use questions when guiding the more content-oriented part of the class discussion' (Flanders 1970: 102). This ratio takes into account events such as lecturing, teachers' questions and the use of practical/real-life examples in lessons. The TQR in this study is 27 per cent; this indicates that teachers across further education colleges asked an 'average' number of questions in the classroom (the TQR across FE will have been significantly lower if you remove a question and answer teaching session from the analysis). The results generally highlight the low frequency of teachers' questions in the classroom discourse.

Teacher response ratio

The teacher response ratio varies across the curriculum areas observed. It ranges from relatively high: 38.8 per cent, 28.6 per cent and 28.1 per cent for humanities/social sciences, the ICT and business studies curriculum respectively, to relatively low: 24.6 and 17.6 per cent for 'other' and maths and sciences respectively. These results indicate that teachers in two of the six curriculum areas observed asked a below 'average' number of questions in the classroom (Flanders suggested a TQR 'average' per cent of 26).

The maths and sciences curriculum produced the lowest TQR (17.7 per cent), well below the further education average. This suggests that teachers in maths and sciences classes are least likely to ask questions often in their lessons. The humanities/social science curriculum area contributed significantly to the overall TQR (38.8 per cent); this suggests that teachers in this curriculum area are more likely to use questions more frequently in lessons than do teachers in other curriculum areas (although the nature of the subjects in this curriculum might have played a part in raising the TQR). Across the qualification areas, the teacher question ratios in A level, GNVQ/AVCE, NVQ and access to HE classes are 29.1 per cent, 21.9 per cent, 27.5 per cent and 54.2 per cent respectively. These results suggest that teachers in three of the four qualification areas asked an 'average' number of questions in the classroom, the exception being teachers in access to HE classes, where the number of questions is significantly higher, due partly to the fact that a teacher used part of lesson time for a question and answer session.

Teacher emphasis on content

The question of how much emphasis teachers placed on content in the classroom discourse was examined by analysing the content cross ratio (CCR). I found in this study a CCR of 69.2 per cent across the further education colleges; this indicates that the subject matter is the focus of classroom discussion and that teachers take a lead and possibly dominant role in discussion, but barely pay attention to motivation-sustaining events such as praise and students' self-expression. It is worth noting that the low frequency per cent reported for 'praising students' in the classroom observations is consistent with the students' rating for teachers' approval and motivation in lessons analysed from the student questionnaire.

The analysis of CCR according to the curriculum areas observed indicates little variation in all but one curriculum area. The content cross ratios of 77.1 per cent, 74.5 per cent, 73.7 per cent and 72.9 per cent, in maths and sciences, business studies, 'other' and the humanities/social sciences curriculum respectively, are all above the further education average except ICT, which produced a CCR of 46.7 per cent. These results mean that teachers in five of the six curriculum areas give significant emphasis to subject matter in classroom discourse and that they are very active and take the lead role in the discussion, but do not give enough attention to motivation (although it is possible that teachers assume they motivate students by talking). The CCR of 46.7 per cent for ICT is well below Flanders' 'mythical' average of 55 per cent; nonetheless, the ICT result suggests a more or less balanced mixture of content (teacher activity) and practical (student activity) expected in subjects such as information technology and computing studies.

The content cross ratios across the four qualification areas are 77.5 per cent, 62.8 per cent, 80 per cent and 80 per cent for A level, GNVQ/AVCE, NVQ and access to HE respectively. The results indicate that teachers in A level, NVQ and access to HE classes are active, take lead role and place significant emphasis on subject matter in the classroom discussion, but pay very little attention to motivation-sustaining events such as praise and allowing students' views and ideas. The CCR for NVQ classes is surprisingly high, given the fact that the qualification emphasizes competence over content. In the GNVQ/AVCE classes, a relatively low CCR is not unexpected, given that the qualification seeks to promote flexibility in assessment. A critical issue highlighted by these findings is that, except in the GNVQ/ACVE classes, there is no significant difference in teachers' emphasis on subject matter in the qualification areas despite their having different aims and assessment structures. These results mirror findings in Bloomer and Hodkinson's (1997) investigation of students' learning experiences in further education, where students reported no real differences in teachers' practices in GNVQ and A level classes.

Teacher reference to real-life situations
Applying classroom knowledge to real life is a means of contextualizing learning and is essential to developing student creativity (Ball 1995; Parnell 1999; Seltzer and Bentley 1999). The average teachers' talk time on citing practical examples or on relating learning to the real world is 3.1 per cent. This result highlights a virtual absence of this feature in classroom discourse in the FE classrooms observed in the study. In the six curriculum areas observed, the results are similar – at the top end are maths and sciences (6.4 per cent) and business studies (4.1 per cent) and at the lower end are 'other' (2.2 per cent), ICT (1.7 per cent), and humanities and social sciences (1.2 per cent). The results on the whole are consistent with

the students' accounts of how often their teacher relates learning to real-life situations. The results underlined the points that have been made in the preceding chapters about the importance of asking practical questions in lessons or relating teaching to real-life situations.

Managing behavioural problems

Effective teaching of the 14–19 year old group is not only about good lesson planning and preparation and delivery: the ability to manage the class effectively is equally important. As already mentioned in the previous chapters, the key to effective classroom management lies in knowing precisely what might have been responsible for students' discipline problems, such as side-chatting and distractions, uncivil language or behaviours that disrupted the learning of other students in the classroom. If you find your students engaging in side-chatting or distraction while you are teaching, you should challenge them, but with concern; it may be that they were finding your presentation difficult to follow. If all that the students were doing was asking each other questions, it may be that you need to encourage them to direct their questions to you or the whole class so that they might receive better answers.

What did the research say about being effective in teaching 14–19 year olds?

It said, and still says, a lot. You need to get your students to ask questions in your lessons; it is a good way to develop students' 'inquiry minds'. You need to identify right from the planning and preparation stage (see chapter 3) how you intend to help your students to raise their levels of self-confidence and ask challenging questions in the classroom. Another message from this research is that you should encourage students to work on their own – to develop individual knowledge application – as much as you encourage them to work in a group – to foster interaction; you should strike a balance between group work and individual student work. Also, encourage your students to take risks and express themselves in coursework, class or homework activities; assure them that they will be rewarded for their creativity. I cannot overstate the need to encourage student creativity in learning and teaching; 14–19 subject specifications now require students to apply knowledge in both familiar and unfamiliar situations (Ogunleye 2006). They also require that students use a range of methods in essay-format coursework. The reason for this requirement is twofold: to discourage teachers from 'teaching to test' and students from 'learning to test'.

Conclusion

In this chapter I have tried to present some of the findings of a recent study into the teaching and learning experiences of students in further education. The findings provide insights into students' and teachers' classroom behaviours and practices, as well as underlining the importance of knowing about these dispositions in your striving for excellence in teaching. The next chapter shows how you can improve your teaching through continuing personal and professional development.

8 Sharpening your teaching skills – continuing professional development

Introduction

This chapter points out the importance of professional development as key to improving teaching practice. It highlights professional development activities such as examining, moderating and verifying vocational assessments. It also highlights the need for personal development in creativity, drawing on research in further education.

Own your professional development

If you are a new lecturer, successful acquisition of a teaching qualification should not be seen as an end in itself, but a means to it; if you are an experienced lecturer, you should continually strive to improve your practice. But whether you are at the beginning or in the middle of your teaching career, continuing professional development is key to *continuing* improvement in your teaching. There are two aspects to a lecturer's continuing professional development – one relates to curriculum development and the other relates to career and future skills development. A study by the Scottish Further Education Funding Council (SFEFC 2005) indicates that a majority of Scottish colleges inspected 'did not address career and future skills development systematically enough'. I'm not suggesting that colleges do not support lecturers, especially those aspiring for programme or curriculum management positions. What I'm suggesting is that your college will not always be able to support your professional development as well as it might want to for some reasons. Those reasons might include inadequate funds allocation for staff development and a low priority 'given to pedagogic skills, in comparison with assessor training' (FEFC 1999). What this means is that you will do well to *own* your continuing development proactively, rather than expect others to provide this for you. One way to do this is to take active interest in your personal and professional development.

Write your annual professional development plan

You should get into the habit of writing your own personal and professional development plan annually and stick with it. A professional development plan is like a road map, which enables you to see well in advance the goals you set out to achieve in the coming year and how you set about achieving your goals at different points in the plan. The survey by the Scottish Further Education Funding Council (SFEFC 2005: 2) found that teachers who keep logs of their professional development activities found the process valuable. As the Scottish Further Education Funding Council put it:

Staff did not generally keep record of their own continuing professional development except those for whom it was an industry requirement. Those who did often valued the process.

There is no standard structure for a professional development plan, but there are basics that you need to include. A simple professional development plan should identify your aims and objectives for the coming year and demonstrate the relevance of these objectives to your needs. An example could be a particular aspect of the syllabus that you noticed students found difficult to understand despite your best effort at varying teaching styles and you do not want your next group to 'experience' a similar problem of understanding. It may also be that you were concerned that external moderators did not often accept your marks and you needed an insight into how moderators moderated to QCA standards. Whatever your goals, a good professional development plan should focus intensely on developing your role in helping students to learn while helping you to improve your professional practice, knowledge and/or qualifications and career/life opportunities. Once you set out your aims and objectives, you then need to identify steps required to achieve those objectives. At the end of each year, it is good practice to reflect on, or to evaluate, your professional development plan before setting new goals for another year.

Forms of professional development

There are a variety of different kinds of professional development: in this chapter, I focus on useful aspects of 14–19 teaching-related development. Professional development geared to improving subject knowledge, teaching skills and knowledge of curriculum development takes many forms; what is important is that you are aware of your needs and how to go about meeting those needs. The following paragraphs highlight a number of time-tested forms of professional development for teachers of 14–19 year olds.

Become an external examiner

As a teacher of 14–19 year olds, there is no better way to enhance your professional credentials than to become an external examiner for one of the unitary examination boards in the UK. The three main English boards – OCR, Edexcel and AQA – between them offer a range of subjects at levels 2 and 3, the equivalent of GCSE and GCE A level respectively, and they continue to recruit examiners. Although your role as an examiner will be primarily to mark examination scripts, the real professional development aspect lies in what is undoubtedly an unparalleled insight you will gain from this into how students from a wide range of abilities approach exam questions and how you, as a lecturer, might improve your teaching in the light of your experience. The role will also provide you with an opportunity to network with teachers from other colleges and much more.

As one examiner put it:

I wanted to get an insight into how credit was given, and being an examiner enabled me to feed information back to my department so that the school [or college] could mark work in the same way as examiners would. It's certainly taught me a lot about what sort of answers get top level marks.

(www.examinerrecruitment.org)

An AQA chief examiner explained:

Many teachers have said, having been to standardizing meetings and been through mark schemes carefully to prepare for marking, that it's the best INSET they could possibly do. They also don't have to pay for doing it, they actually get paid for doing it. I think it is a huge benefit and that has been confirmed by many teachers.

(*AQA Examiner* Autumn 2005: 3)

One AQA examiner recounted:

The insight I gained when I first became an examiner made a real difference to my teaching. First-hand experience of seeing work from a range of candidates and centres enabled me to pitch my teaching at just the right level and to focus on aspects where candidates tend to under-perform. I also gained a much greater understanding of the specification and how to apply the assessment criteria to candidates' work.

(www.aqa.org.uk)

When you stand before your students, they know you are talking from the position of being both a teacher and an examiner; when you organize sessions on examination techniques, they are more likely to hang on to your every word.

The examination marking process
As you probably know, external examinations for many 14–19 year olds take place annually between January and February and between May and June. The main marking period for most examiners is between the middle of June and early July. The examination process is relatively straightforward: candidates complete the examination; centres send scripts allocated to you directly to your home address (or via the Internet if you are trained to mark scripts online). In the meantime, you will attend an examiners' standardizing meeting, which is compulsory. The objective of the standardizing meeting is to get everyone to mark to the same standard as the chief examiner, to discuss mark schemes and receive guidance on marking. The standardizing meeting provides you with an opportunity to ask your team leader questions relating to the marking. It also provides an opportunity to ask your assessment leader questions relating to administration. At the end of the meeting, you will go home with a sample of 'standardized' scripts to mark alongside a few live scripts and report your marks to your team leader, usually within 3–5 days. You will get a go-ahead to continue to mark if your team leader is satisfied with your marking. Your team leader will ask for a second or even a third sample of marked scripts

at some points during the marking period to monitor standards. Some exam boards may require that you submit your marks by telephone or by post at regular intervals during the marking period. Once you have finished with all your marking, you will return the marked scripts to the exam board. The exam board will complete the examination process with the publication of the results in August.

Become an external moderator

The work of a moderator is similar to that of an examiner in many respects – an examiner marks exam papers while a moderator moderates a unit of coursework and writes a report on the moderation of each centre to which he or she is allocated. An external moderator does not have to accept marks awarded by the centre, but may make recommendations for new marks. Every new examiner and moderator will receive training prior to, or at, the standardizing meeting.

Listen to this testimony by a moderator:

The professional development opportunities were obvious from the start: making such a number of new professional relationships; getting close to the examination/moderation system bring huge benefits to my teaching which I was able to share with my departments. Lots of doors opened for me because of my involvement as a moderator: I have been able to get involved with syllabus/specification development and the subsequent teacher-support meetings that have followed.

(*AQA Examiner* Autumn 2005: 12)

Become an external verifier

An external verifier is a guardian and an upholder of standards in national vocational qualifications such as NVQs. If you teach mainly vocational courses, becoming an external verifier is a logical step to take in your professional development. You need not have any previous experience; as a lecturer of NVQ units you will have already demonstrated occupational competence in your subject area and your experience as a vocational assessor and internal verifier should provide a basis for the role of an external verifier. You will receive training and other support from your exam board to help you settle into the role.

Engage in action research

If you were the type of lecturer who likes to find answers to class-room challenges, you should consider engaging in action research to improve your professional practice. Action research is particularly recommended if you want to be close to what is being studied. If you want to take the action research challenge, the first thing is knowing what to do at the planning stage; this will comprise activities such as identifying a research topic, stating research problems or questions, reading relevant literature, identifying a research methodology and projecting a research timeline. The second is knowing what to do at the implementation stage; this will consist of activities such as further reading, revision of research questions, and data collection. The third is knowing what to do at the data analysis or presentation stage; this is where you probe, interrogate or try to make sense of the data collected and attempt to discuss your work in the light of other work on the subject. At this stage, your research findings should illuminate the research questions or support what is already known on the subject. Although there is no clear evidence to suggest that all forms of action research are powerful enough to lead automatically to improved professional development of the teacher–researcher, Cousin (2005: 141), in a report on action research development projects in 87 further education colleges, notes a link 'between the morale of staff and their ability to be self–reflective'.

Present your work to colleagues

Once you have completed your research, don't keep the findings to yourself; explore ways to present your findings to your colleagues. With the permission of college managers, you can organize a seminar to which you invite colleagues. One way to get people to come along is to organize the seminar around lunch-time and provide light refreshments (check beforehand if your college will pick up the hospitality bill). If you think there is something in your findings that other people outside your college should know about, then get in touch with the Learning and Skills Network (LSN); it has contacts in the post–16 Learning and Skills Research Network which provides a forum for practitioners like you to present their work. Other organizations also worth contacting are the Further Education Research Association and the Society for Research into

Higher Education HE–FE National Network as well as the British Educational Research Association SIG (Special Interest Group) on Post-Compulsory Education Research (see webpage resources in the Appendix).

Become an 'in-house' expert on 14–19 provision

If you would like to impress colleagues and senior managers alike with your knowledge of the 14–19 policy agenda, you should consider keeping yourself continual up to date on the subject. There is nothing like teaching a programme area in which you know a great deal about the issues that informed the government's policy agenda. There is also nothing like becoming an 'in-house' expert on 14–19 provision whose opinions senior managers take very seriously. It doesn't take too much effort to get into the routine – all you need is to develop a love for reading and writing up your notes. Keep an eye on both local and national government policy initiatives relating to 14–19 curriculum and qualifications as well as research reports on the subject. Your knowledge of 14–19 provision will help you to design and deliver courses that are 'fit for the purpose', to examine the impact of any new policy on learning and teaching, and to monitor research to identify evidence of good practice that can be used to improve teaching and learning. It is what continuing professional development should be all about.

Personal development in creativity

I believe some of the best personal and professional development activities are those that focus on developing teachers' creativity. How teachers nourish their creativity varies: teachers in Ogunleye (2002) cited networking with colleagues outside college as an important source of their creativity; vocational teachers cited their professional contacts in the industry as nourishing agents of their creativity. General staff development programmes such as in-house training and outside courses, conferences, seminars, lectures, talks and classroom observations; inviting outside experts to give talks or to demonstrate new learning aids and equipment, were all said to aid their creativity. As this teacher of A level biology put it:

Each year I find a top scientist from the local university and he comes and (literally) takes the laboratory over for a whole day. He brings all the modern equipment and loads the whole thing, ready to go. He is at the forefront on the subject and I want more of that – to watch him in the lab, to learn from him.

Another important source of 'creativity nourishment' for teachers is the classroom – via feeding on students' ideas, according to this teacher of A level media studies:

The worst lessons to me are the ones where you hadn't any idea from the students, because when you hear other people's ideas, you challenge yours and that in itself is creativity [a creative exercise].

A teacher of A level sociology underlined how student feedback has encouraged the teaching staff to take risks [risk-taking is a creative attribute]:

It is feedback from lessons, really. We feedback all the time and we are not afraid to take risks. The feedback encourages us [the teachers] to take risks.

Personal interests and hobbies – such as going to the theatre, museums, watching documentaries on television – and leisure-time research, as part of lesson planning and preparation, were cited as nourishing agents of teachers' creativity, as this teacher of NVQ administration explained:

On the Sunday evening I go to bed with all the papers and I research articles in the papers that I know will be relevant to my different teaching. One student said to me: 'Oh Miss, you have a sad life!'

Despite the 'frequent' policy changes in the further education sector that are often cited as a constraint to student creativity, a science teacher said she found stimulus in such changes:

Because everything changes every couple of years or so, that gets you to do new things and face new challenges (even though it can be tiring sometimes). So, you know, things never get stale.

The teachers' personal development in creativity includes surfing the Internet for ideas and feeding off lesson ideas from colleagues; maintaining a positive mind and approach to work, risk-taking, good relationships with students; interest in the subject specialism, writing assignments; regular self-evaluation and review of teaching methods and practices, as this teacher of AVCE ICT explained:

Nourishing creativity is one thing, to keep it working is another thing. I have always found that once you have actually done an activity you can say that has worked. I tend to ask myself what can I do to make it even better. I probably try again in a slight different format in a different class. Each time you do it, you build on it, and each time you try and evaluate after each time – always trying to improve it and make it better.

Conclusion

In this chapter, I have tried to encourage you to take active interest in your own professional development, noting that, despite your employer's best intentions, experience suggests that constraints of resources – money in particular – often make it difficult to turn best intentions into reality. This explains why you need to draw up your own personal and professional development plan; write up and update the plan year after year as your needs develop or change. There are many ways you can develop yourself – you can become an examiner in your subject, to gain insight into the marking process and to pick up useful tips for your students. The three English examination boards between them offer a diverse range of subjects; one of these subjects will most likely interest you. Get involved; improve yourself professionally, and earn an extra income. Alternatively, keep abreast of developments in the 14–19 curriculum and elevate your interest to an art form.

Table 8.1 Sample professional development plan

Professional Development Plan: .... My Name: .... Year: 2006–7

Date	Development activity	Development aims/ objectives	Progress/evaluation	Outcome/impact of activity/other comments
15 June 2007	External examining activity	To become an external examiner for OCR in AS sociology.	Successful appointment; successful induction. Had a good standardizing meeting.	I gained insight into how students from a wide range of abilities approached exam questions and into how my own students' performance can be improved.
28 June 2007	Action research and professional networking with research group: LSRN London and South-east Network meeting in London	1. To present my research findings at the LSRN annual conference, summer 2008. 2. Aim to gain more funding for my research.	1. Aim 1 from last year achieved! Gained £1,000 from staff development budget for my research on Observations of 14–16 Teaching in FE in ICT Classrooms. 2. The overall research plan is complete, data being collected.	Enjoyed the meeting, especially learning about communities of practice drawing on the work of Jean Lave and Etienne Wenger.

9 Summary – effective teaching of 14–19 students in FE

Introduction

This chapter summarizes some of the main teaching techniques, ideas and suggestions discussed in the foregoing chapters.

Preparing to teach 14–19 students – lesson planning and preparation

The three characteristics of lesson planning and preparation are knowledge, confidence and passion; they are key to effective lesson delivery. There is little doubt that FE lecturers have specialist knowledge of their subjects. There is also little doubt that lecturers have passion for their subjects and are confident about delivering them. What is in doubt is whether lecturers fully appreciate the relationships between the three characteristics and whether they manifest them in lesson planning. Your self-confidence and passion for your subject will determine the extent of your lesson planning and preparation; it will make a difference in the way you design or structure your lesson plan, in the way you source, organize and write up teaching and learning materials and in the way you present your lesson. Confidence at all the stages of teaching and learning will include confidence to deliver the subject, to use the teaching or instructional materials and to control or manage the class. Students can spot a confidence-lacking teacher delivering a particularly difficult topic, especially when the teacher's style of delivery made them nod off in lesson. A joined-up thinking in KCP (knowledge, confidence and passion) in lesson planning and preparation will enable you to anticipate aspects of the lesson with which students are likely to find difficulty; it will enable you to prepare students beforehand by identifying and specifying possible 'turn-off' or 'nodding-off' points in lessons – by thinking through other ways of presenting difficult bits to students, with passion. Let your passion inform the way you write or organize learning material – do this by identifying potentially frustrating moments that are unavoidable in lessons. You can then plan in advance 'hook points' that can sustain students' interest. 'Hook points' in a lesson plan might include asking students, individually, questions on the background information search that you have asked them to collect in the previous lesson.

Keys to effective teaching of 14–16 year olds

There are four attributes that I found in highly successful teachers of 14–16 year olds, which might have helped their teaching. The first is that they went out of their way to help students to manage the transition from school to college. The second attribute I found is that highly successful teachers made students see the point of coming to college for vocational learning. 14–16 year olds come to college full of expectations to learn in a new, bigger environment as well as to experience different approaches to teaching and learning. The third attribute is that highly successful teachers made it a duty to meet with students informally prior to their first lesson. The fourth attribute – and probably the most important – that I found in highly successful teachers is that they liked to take the creative challenge. As a creative teacher, you will reflect on your teaching techniques and you will constantly seek a new, better way to deliver your lessons. Here are some tips for effective teaching of 14–16 year olds.

Use creative lesson introductions or starters
Your lesson starter should serve a dual purpose: to introduce the lesson and at the same time whet the students' appetite for it. Using starters gives you the flexibility to begin your lesson right away without having to wait for the whole group to arrive. When students come into a lesson, they know that there is always an activity or a discussion they can join in.

Vary the pace of your lesson
Think of the lesson pace as the 'speed' of the lesson in a period. This will include how long you intend to spend on 'teacher

activity' such as presentation and questioning; on 'student activity' such as group work, individual work, questioning, students' practice and application of newly taught skills and knowledge.

Challenge your students

If students do not find your first few lessons challenging enough, they will soon label your session 'boring' and it will be a hard job getting them to tune in again in subsequent ones. You can challenge students on four fronts: in the way you present lessons, in the way you set class work, in the way you set homework and by asking questions or setting them activities that arouse interest for the subject and the learning process.

Develop good questioning skills

Good questioning skills are characteristics of effective teaching, which can help to stimulate students' creative thinking. Ask questions according to the particular demands of the topic you are teaching; ask open-ended or divergent questions if you desire to develop student enquiry and creative thinking. You can use questioning to challenge or motivate students to learn, to reinforce teaching, to check on the students' progress and to manage and control the classroom.

Relate learning to the real world

To relate learning to a real-world context is to use community and workplace problems to underpin your teaching. Highly successful teachers try to make students see the point of turning up for lessons by connecting learning to the world around their students.

Use humour to a good effect

Young learners like lecturers who 'use jokes' in lessons. To use humour to a good effect, you need to ensure that the joke relates to the topic that is being taught. You should never use humour to embarrass students or to make sarcastic remarks about them.

Vary teaching styles

Make it a habit to vary your teaching styles in *every* lesson. Use teacher exposition or whole-class teaching, for example if you are introducing a new topic. Get students to work individually and go round the class to offer one-to-one support, for example if they need to develop particular technical skills; encourage small-team discussion where you require divergent answers to particular questions or class tasks.

Be sensitive to students' needs

Key Stage 4 students are quite aware of their personalities and can be sensitive to their environment. Be sensitive to their individual and collective needs and appreciate them. Respect and value their opinions and have high expectations of them.

Keep to time

Keep to time and manage it well during lessons. If you ask students to attempt class activities, say precisely how many minutes you want them to use to complete the activities.

Manage behaviours

Highly successful teachers manage students' behaviours by being firm, but friendly, to get their attention. They do not shout nor get angry with students, neither do they have a template response to every behaviour situation in their lessons.

Prepare students for the next lesson

Whet the appetites of the students for their next lesson. Use the closing section of today's lesson to introduce the students to new vocabulary or technical information that they might need to learn for the next lesson; talk them through it, explain its relevance and demonstrate how the topic relates to real-life situations.

Effective teaching of 16–19 year olds

Methods used in teaching 14–16 year olds can also be applied or adapted for use in teaching 16–19 year olds as well as in teaching students aged 19 and over; some of these methods are highlighted below.

Make good use of questioning

Questioning is at the heart of teaching, but a good use of the questioning technique is more than asking questions frequently in lessons. Use a mixture of open-ended and closed questions to get your students actively involved in the classroom. A teacher of a 16–19 group I observed used puzzles and paradoxes, in the form of questions, to tease out responses from his students. The technique worked – it encouraged the students to think through before answering the teacher's questions. Identify what works best for your own group.

Pre-teach subject vocabulary terms
Too often as teachers we try to load students with new learning or material before mastering the basics of the subject or the topic we teach. Pre-teach the basics.

Connect learning to the real world
As mentioned above you can aid student knowledge application and knowledge transformation by putting students' prior know-ledge into context or by relating learning to real-life situations. One way to do this is to provide opportunities for students to 'simulate' a real-life situation or problem in the classroom.

Raise confidence
Raising student confidence is key to engaging 16–19 year olds in learning. Help your students to develop self-confidence in your class. Start with student activities. In setting written activities, ask relatively easy questions at the beginning and ask more challenging questions as the students progress in the activities.

Frequent feedback
When you give students tasks to do in lesson, go round the class and mark as many students' answers as possible. Students need to know how they are doing now and then. If you must collect their work to mark outside lesson because of time constraints, ensure that students receive feedback on their work as soon as you can possibly turn it around.

Vary teaching styles
Vary your teaching styles. Provide opportunities for group work as well as encouraging students to work individually in situations where you want to develop individual application of knowledge.

Experiment with problem-solving teaching styles. You can also experiment with reading assignments. Students can be encouraged to learn the history of the subject to facilitate 'bonds' between the students and the subject.

Make your lesson a haven of activities

A significant part of your lesson should be activity-based. A good lesson should be a beehive of learning activities – 85 to 90 per cent of your lesson time should be used for classroom activities that may consist of student presentation, question and answer, written or oral discussions.

Embed ICT in your lessons

Make it a habit to use information and communication technology in your teaching as regularly and as appropriately as possible. Computer graphics, animation and computer simulation may be used, for example, to teach students whose cognitive disposition might not favour learning in traditional classroom settings.

Effective teaching of a 14–19 mixed group

The following sections highlight some of the techniques you might use to teach a mixed-age class.

Welcome students with a smile

Make eye contact with students as they come into the class and welcome them with an assuring beam. When students come late to lesson, challenge them with concern, but avoid confrontation. As students come into the class don't keep the 'early birds' waiting for the rest of the group; use lesson starters discussed above to arouse and sustain students' interest while you wait for others to arrive.

Use your voice effectively

You need good voice projection skills to teach a mixed class effectively. Project your voice effectively by talking to students with your head up if you are standing in front facing the class. Get the tonal balance of your voice right – it should not be too loud, nor should it be too low. Depending on the size and layout of the classroom, try to move around as you speak and ask questions intermittently to check students' knowledge. Effective use of your voice will increase your confidence in your ability to communicate.

Avoid asking students to copy notes from the whiteboard

You may use the whiteboard or overhead projector to outline the lesson aims and objectives, but avoid asking students to copy long notes from the whiteboard or overhead projector even if it is something that your 14–16 year olds have become used to in school. This practice may not be suitable for your 16–19 group. Use information handouts or sheets for the mixed group, but ensure that the handout is simplified for the 14–16 group, yet detailed enough for the 16–19 group.

Develop group cohesiveness

One way to develop group cohesiveness is to organize a pre-lesson session where the whole group is made to engage in practical discussions. Use well-thought-out, practical questions which allow students to 'own' the discussions; for instance, you may ask questions that require students to use their personal experiences as a basis for their answers. Another way to develop a spirit of cooperation across the age groups is to divide up the class for lesson activities, presentations or investigative activities. Assign students into groups using participation in unusual interests or hobbies as a group selection technique.

Encourage students to take responsibility for their own learning

Your 14–16 year old students are used to being led by the teacher and may take their time settling into the college environment; sometimes they might not be particularly keen to take responsibility for their learning. As the students adjust to their new environment and grapple with new concepts of learning, do everything possible to help them to learn. Your 16–19 year olds should be clear about what you expect from them: this will include an acceptance that they take responsibility for their own learning.

Sustain students' interest

If you have a double-lesson period, ensure that you pack the lesson with a variety of activities for each of the student groups. This means using variable teaching methods; depending on your subject, whole-class teaching, group teaching and one-to-one teaching can all be integrated and used in a double-period session. You can also vary class activities within a particular age group by not giving every student the same tasks to do at the same time. It might also be useful to use colour markers to write key points or technical terms on the whiteboard. The use of colour markers along with the 'traditional' black colour markers is said to 'catch' the attention of younger learners or 'fascinate' older learners. Try also to use different learning aids in every lesson: you can use pictorial representations, symbols, objects, diagrams, etc. and embed some of these in your lessons.

Relate teaching to the world around students

14–16 year olds want to connect to their subjects as do 16–19 year olds; by 'connecting' they mean demonstrating a subject's real-life relevance or application. The use of real-life problems will help your students to interact with the real world.

Praise students regularly in lessons

Many students like to take a step at a time – when answering teachers' questions or when attempting class or homework activities – and they want to be sure each step is 'right' before they take the next. They need help from you to raise their self-confidence to participate in lesson. So let the students know they are making progress, praise the smallest positive step.

Adapt learning material to meet every student's needs

Although you may prefer to use standard textbooks such as the recommended subject-specific textbooks for your class, you should not assume that these books will meet the needs of every student; there will be some students who will find it difficult to read and understand standard textbooks. You will do well to supplement textbooks with tailored handouts or worksheets to meet the needs of weaker students.

Provide clearer information to students about their coursework

14–19 year old students want clearer, unambiguous information about their coursework. When you give students coursework, include enough pointers on how to go about doing it; encourage them to show you their work in draft form before they submit formally. Your students will appreciate your commitment towards their studies.

Use homework effectively
Use homework to reinforce student learning. Ensure that worksheets and learning materials are differentiated, with homework activities clearly marked for the 14–16 group. Set homework also for the 16–19 group to check and reinforce their learning. Ensure that you mark the students' work and give them timely feedback. The students will form their own opinion about your professionalism if you take too much time to mark their work and feed back to them. Next time they may not be too keen to turn in their work on time.

Keys to effective teaching of 14–19 students – message from research

The main message from empirical studies into teaching and learning in 16–19 education is that you need to get your students to ask questions in your lessons; it is a good way to develop a student 'enquiry mind'. You need to identify right from the planning and preparation stage (see chapter 3) how you intend to help your students to raise their self-confidence and ask challenging questions in the classroom. Additionally, you should encourage students to work on their own – to develop individual knowledge application – as much as you encourage them to work in a group – to foster interaction; you should strike a balance between group work and individual student work. Also, encourage your students to take risks and express themselves in coursework, class or homework activities; assure them that they will be rewarded for their creativity.

Sharpening your teaching skills – continuing professional development

Continuing professional development is key to continuing improvement in your teaching. Get into the habit of writing your own personal and professional development plan annually and stick with it. A simple professional development plan should identify your aims and objectives for the coming year and demonstrate the relevance of these objectives to your needs. Whatever your goals, a good professional development plan should focus intensely on helping students to learn while helping you to improve your professional practice. Once you set out your aims and objectives, you then need to identify the steps required to achieve those objectives. At the end of each year, it is good practice to reflect on, or to evaluate, your professional development plan before setting new goals for another year.

Forms of professional development

The following paragraphs highlight a number of time-tested forms of professional development for teachers of 14–19 year olds.

Become an external examiner

As a teacher of 14–19 year olds, there is no better way to enhance your professional credentials than to become an external examiner. Although your role as an examiner will be primarily to mark examination scripts, the real professional development aspect lies in what is undoubtedly an unparalleled insight you will have into how students from a wide range of abilities approached exam questions and how you, as a lecturer, might improve your teaching in the light of your experience.

Become an external moderator

The work of a moderator is similar to that of an examiner in many respects – an examiner marks exam papers while a moderator moderates a unit of coursework and writes a report on the moderation of each centre to which he or she is allocated. Every new examiner and moderator will receive training prior to, or at, the standardizing meeting.

Become an external verifier

An external verifier is a guardian and an upholder of standards in national vocational qualifications such as NVQs. You need not have any previous experience; as a lecturer of NVQ units, you will have already demonstrated occupational competence in your subject area and your experience as a vocational assessor and internal verifier should provide a basis for the role of an external verifier.

Engage in action research

If you are the type of lecturer that likes to find answers to classroom challenges, you should consider engaging in action research to improve your professional practice. Once you have completed your research, don't keep the findings to yourself; explore ways to present your findings to your colleagues. With the permission of college managers, you can organize a seminar to which you invite colleagues.

Become an 'in-house' expert on 14–19 provision

There is nothing like becoming an 'in-house' expert on 14–19 provision whose opinions senior managers take very seriously. It doesn't take too much effort to get into the routine – all you need is to develop a love for reading and writing up your notes. Keep an eye on both local and national government policy initiatives relating to 14–19 curriculum and qualifications as well as research reports on the subject.

Personal development in creativity

I believe some of the best personal and professional development activities are those that focus on developing teachers' creativity. How teachers nourish their creativity varies: teachers in my early work (Ogunleye 2002) cited networking with colleagues outside college as an important source of their creativity; vocational teachers cited their professional contacts in the industry as nourishing agents of their creativity. General staff development programmes such as in-house training and outside courses, conferences, seminars, lectures, talks and classroom observations; inviting outside experts to give talks or to demonstrate new learning aids and equipment, were all said to aid their creativity. Personal interests and hobbies – such as going to the theatre, museums, watching documentaries on television – and leisure-time research, as part of lesson planning and preparation, were cited as nourishing agents of their creativity. The teachers' personal development in creativity also includes surfing the Internet for ideas and feeding off lesson ideas from colleagues; maintaining a positive mind and approach to work, risk-taking, good relationships with students; interest in subject specialism, writing assignments; regular self-evaluation and review of teaching methods and practices.

Conclusion

The aim of this book is to help you to become an effective teacher of 14–19 year olds. I have always believed that, as teachers, we should continue to strive for excellence in our teaching whatever stage we are at in our career; being effective in your teaching can make a world of difference to students' learning. If students believe (or feel) they are learning in your class they will see the point of turning up regularly for your lessons. More so, at a time when the issue of student retention has become a recurring feature in further education, it is important you ensure that students do not drop out of your class because of your teaching approach. If you adopt, adapt or apply the teaching techniques (and the suggested professional development practice) discussed above you certainly should not find yourself in a situation where students would find your teaching uninteresting. I would recommend every one of the techniques discussed above to you; apply them daily as you strive for excellence in your teaching. I thank you for reading this far and I wish you good luck in your teaching and professional development.

References and further reading

Ainley, P. (2003) 'Towards a seamless web or a new tertiary tripartism? The emerging shape of post-14 education and training in England', *British Journal of Educational Studies* 51(4): 390–407.

Allan, J. and Gartside, P. (1989) 'Induction into further education', *SCRE Spotlights*, Edinburgh: The Scottish Council for Research in Education.

AQA (2005) *AQA Examiner* newsletter, Autumn, Guildford: Assessment and Qualifications Alliance.

Audit Commission/Ofsted (1993) *Unfinished Business: Full-time Educational Courses for 16–19 Year Olds*, London: HMSO.

Ball, S. (1995) 'Enriching student learning through innovative real-life exercises', *Education and Training* 37(4): 18–25. Bradford: Bradford University Press.

Bloomer, M. and Hodkinson, P. (1997) *Moving into FE: The Voices of the Learner*, London: FEDA.

Cackowski, Z. (1969) 'A creative problem-solving process', *Journal of Creative Behaviour* 3(3): 185–93.

Campbell, M. (2003) 'The skills gap: smart moves', *Guardian Education Weekly*, 2 December, p.18.

Cantor, J. A. (1992) *Apprenticeship and Community Colleges: Collaborations for Tomorrow's Workforce*, Final report, Bronx: Lehman College, City University of New York.

Cantor, L, Roborts, L. and Pratley, B. (1995) *A Guide to Further Education in England and Wales*, London: Cassell Education.

Chandhari, V. S. (1975) 'Questioning and creative teaching: a research perspective', *Journal of Creative Behaviour* 9(1): 30–4.

Cousin, S. (2005) 'Action research', in Hillier, Y. and Thompson, A. (eds) *Readings in Post-Compulsory Education*, London: Continuum.

Cranton, P. (1992) *Working with Adult Learners*, Toronto, ON: Wall & Emerson.

Cripps, S. (2002) *Further Education: Government's Discourse Policy and Practice*. Aldershot: Ashgate.

Cropley, A. J. (2001) *Creativity in Education and Learning: A Guide for Teachers and Educators*, London: Kogan Page.

Curtis, P. (2004) 'Teachers welcome Tomlinson proposals', *Guardian*, 17 February (accessed 24 July 2006 from http://education.guardian-.co.uk/thebaccalaureate/story/0,,1150018,00.html).

Curzon, L. B. (1997) *Teaching in Further Education: An outline of Principles and Practice*, London: Cassell Education.

Davies, H. (2002) *A Review of Enterprise and the Economy in Education*, London: HMSO.

Davies, T. (2000) 'Confidence! Its role in the creative teaching and learning of design and technology', *Journal of Technology Education* 12(1) (accessed 10 August 2006 from http://scholar.lib.vt.edu/ejournals/JTE/v12nl/davies.html).

Dearing, R. (1996) *Review of Qualifications for 16–19 Year Olds*, London: SCAA.

DfEE (1996a) *Equipping Young People for Working Life: A Consultative Document on Improving Employability through the 14–16 Curriculum*, London: HMSO.

DfEE (1996b) *Learning to Compete: Education and Training for 14–19 Year Olds*, White Paper, London: HMSO.

DfEE (1997) *Qualifying for Success*, London: HMSO.

DfEE (1999) *All Our Futures: Creativity, Culture and Education*, National Advisory Committee on Creativity, Culture and Education, London: HMSO.

DfES (2001) *Schools Achieving Success*, White Paper, London: HMSO.

DfES (2002) *14–19: Extending Opportunities, Raising Standards*, Green Paper, London: HMSO.

DfES (2003a) *14–19: Opportunity and Excellence*, White Paper, London: HMSO.

DfES (2003b) *21st Century Skills: Realising Our Potential, Individuals, Employers, Nation*, London: HMSO.

DfES (2004a) *Department for Education and Skills: Five-Year Strategy for Children and Learners*, London: HMSO.

DfES (2004b) *Making Mathematics Count: The Report of Professor Adrian Smith's Inquiry into Post-14 Mathematics Education*, London: DfES.

DfES (2005) *14–19 Education and Skills*, White Paper, London: HMSO.

DfET/DTI (2001) *Opportunity for All in a World of Change*, London: Department for Education and Training/Department of Trade and Industry.

Edexcel Foundation (1999, February), flyer: *NVQ Beauty Therapy*, Mansfield: Edexcel Publications.

FEFC (1997) *Quality and Standards in Further Education in England 1996–97*, Coventry: FEFC.

FEFC (1999) *Professional Development in Further Education in England 1998–99*, Coventry: FEFC.

FEU (1987) *Creative and Arts Activities in Further Education: A Discussion Paper*, London: Further Education Unit.

Flanders, N. A. (1970) *Analysing Teaching Behaviour*, Reading, MA: Addison-Wesley.

Frankel, A. and Reeves, F. (1996) *The FE Curriculum*, Wolverhampton: Bilston College Publications.

Golden, S., O'Donnell, L., Benton, T. and Rudd, P. (2005) *Evaluation of Increased Flexibility for 14 to 16 Year Olds Programme: Outcomes for the First Cohort* (DfES Research Report 668), London: DfES.

Green, A. (1997) 'Core skills, general education and qualifications in post–16 education', in Spours, K. (ed.) *Dearing and Beyond 14–16 Qualification, Frameworks and Systems*, London: Kogan Page.

Higham, J., Haynes, G., Wragg, C. and Yeomans, D. (2004) *14–19 Pathfinders: An Evaluation of the First Year*, London: DfES.

Hodgson, A. and Spours, K. (2002) 'Increasing demand for higher education in the longer term: the role of 14+ qualifications and curriculum reform', in Hayton, A. and Paczuska, A. (eds) *Access, Participation and Higher Education*, London: Kogan Page.

Hodgson, A. and Spours, K. (2005) 'The learner experience of Curriculum 2000: implications for the reform of 14–19 education in England', *Journal of Education Policy* 20(1): 101–18.

James, D. (1999) 'A creative approach to teaching methods', in Ashcroft, J. and James, D. (eds) *The creative Professional. Learning to Teach 14–19 Year-Olds*, London: Falmer Press.

Jane, K., Lloyd, J. K., Braund, M., Crebbin, C. and Phipps, R. (2000) 'Primary teachers' confidence about and understanding of process skills', *Teacher Development* 4(3): 353–70.

Jones, T. P. (1972) *Creative Learning in Perspective*, London: University of London Press.

Kearsley, G. (1996) *Andragogy (M. Knowles)*, Washington, DC: George Washington University (http//gwis2.circ.gwu.edu/~kearsley/knowles.html).

Keep, E. (2003) 'The skills gap: no problem', *Guardian Education Weekly*, 16 December, p.16.

Kingston, P. (2003) 'Method madness: some education targets are more fantasy than fact', *Guardian Education Weekly*, 23 September, p.51.

Knowles, M. S. (1975) *Self-Directed Learning. A Guide for Learners and Teachers*, Englewood Cliffs, NJ: Prentice Hall/Cambridge University Press.

Knowles, M. S. *et al.* (1984) *Andragogy in Action: Applying Modern Principles of Adult Education*, San Francisco: Jossey Bass.

Labelle, B. (1974) 'Creative problem-solving techniques in nursing', *Journal of Creative Behaviour* 8(1): 55–66.

Lloyd, J. K., Braund, M., Crebbin, C. and Phipps, R. (2000) 'Primary teachers' confidence about and understanding of process skills', *Teacher Development* 6(3): 353–69.

LSDA (2002) *An Analysis of the Provision of Alternative, non School-Based Learning Activities for 14–16 Year Olds in Nottinghamshire*, London: Learning and Skills Development Agency.

McFarlane, A. E. (1993) *Data Logging in Science* (video and booklet), Coventry: NCET.

Miliband, D. (2003) '14–19: Opportunity and excellence – developing the Key Stage 4 curriculum', response from Schools' Minister, David Miliband, to Qualifications and Curriculum Authority's advice, dated 1 May 2003, London: DfES.

Minton, D. (2005) *Teaching Skills in Further and Adult Education* (3rd edn), London: Thomson Learning.

Moore, M. G. and Kearsely, G. (1996) *Distance Education: A Systems View*, Belmont, CA: Wadsworth.

Morris, E. (2002) Foreword, *14–19: Extending Opportunities, Raising Standards*, London: HMSO.

NCVQ (1995) *BTEC GNVQs Specifications: Engineering Advanced*, GNVQ Mandatory and Core Skills Units, National Council for Vocational Qualifications.

Norrington, J. and Hayday, S. (2002) '14–16: getting it right', *FeNow*, Spring.

Ofsted (2003a) *14 to 19 Area Inspection, Sandwell*, http://www.ofsted. gov.uk/reports/ (accessed 15 September 2003).

Ofsted (2003b, July) *Supporting 14 to 19 Education: Evidence from the Work of 12 LEAs*, HMI 586, e-publication, http://www.ofsted.gov.uk/reports/ (accessed 15 September 2003).

Ogunleye, J. (2000) 'Facilitating creativity in further education: a key to improving retention in 16–19 full-time courses', *Goldsmiths Journal of Education* 2(2): 13–24.

Ogunleye, J. (2002) 'An investigation of curriculum arrangements fostering creativity in post-compulsory education and training', PhD thesis, University of Greenwich, London.

Ogunleye, J. (2003) 'Mt Hood Community College and Reynolds High School: a research report', a report by the author to the Administrators of Mt Hood Community College and Reynolds High School, Gresham, OR following a research visit to the two schools.

Ogunleye, J. (2006) 'A review and analysis of assessment objectives of academic and vocational qualifications in English further education, with particular reference to creativity', *Journal of Education and Work* 19(1): 95–104.

Ogunleye, J. and McNay, I. (2005) *The Seacole Centre: A Research Report*, London: The Learning Trust/The Community College Hackney.

Painter, J. (1996) 'Questioning techniques for gifted students', The Australian Association for the Education of the Gifted and Talented (http//www.nexus.edu.au/teachstud/gat/painter.htm).

Parnell, D. (1999) 'Connecting learning to real world produces excellence', *The Greenville News*, 19 May, Greenville, SC (www.dropoutprevention.org/featuredart/feat.htm).

Pratt, H. (1981) 'Science education in the elementary school', in Harms, N. and Yager, R. (eds) *What Research Says to the Science Teacher* (Vol. 3: 73–93), Washington, DC: National Science Teachers Association.

QCA (2003) *Changes to the Key Stage 4 Curriculum: Guidance for implementation from September 2004*, London: Qualifications and Curriculum Authority, QCA/03/1167 (www.qca.org.uk).

QCA (2004) *New Thinking for Reform*, London: Qualifications and Curriculum Authority, QCA/04/1306 (www.qca.org.uk).

Sale, D. (2004) 'Making your teaching creative and interesting', *CDTLink* (a triannual publication of the Centre for development of Teaching and Learning of the National University of Singapore) 8(2): 11.

Seltzer, K. and Bentley, T. (1999) *The Creative Age: Knowledge and Skills for the New Economy*, London: Demos.

SFEFC (2005) *Initial and continuing staff development for teaching staff in Scottish further education colleges*, a report by HM Inspectors of Education for the Scottish Further Education Council (http://www.hmie.gov.uk/).

Social Exclusion Unit (1999) *Bridging the gap: new opportunities for 16–18 year-olds not in education, employment or training*, Cm 4405, London: HMSO.

Sproson, B. (2003) 'Solution or smoke screen? The use of further education colleges in making KS4 provision for difficult to manage (DM2) students', *Support for Learning* 18(1): 18–23.

Stevenson, R. B. (1990) 'Engagement and cognitive challenge in thoughtful social studies classes: a study of student perspectives', *Journal of Curriculum Studies* 22(4): 329–42.

Tomlinson Report (2004) *14–19 Curriculum and Qualifications Reform: Final Report of the Working Group on 14–19 Reform*, London: DfES.

Wilhelm, J. D., Baker, T. N. and Dube, J. (2001) *Strategic Reading: Guiding Students to Lifelong Literacy 6–12*, Portsmouth, NH: Heinemann.

Appendix: webpage resources

Government agenda on 14–19 education and training
Department for Education and Skills – http://www.dfes.gov.uk/
You will find almost everything you need on this site including links to other pages.
Further education – http://www.dfes.gov.uk/furthereducation/
Post–16 and lifelong learning – http://www.lifelonglearning. co.uk/z-post16.htm

Teaching and learning and curriculum and arrangements
Learn more about changes to KS4 curriculum – http://www.qca. org.uk/
Learn more about curriculum arrangements and qualifications framework for the 14–19 phase.
Vocational learning – http://www.vocationallearning.org.uk/
This is a very useful site for lecturers and practitioners of 14–19 education and training. The site 'provides resources, materials, publications and information from the Vocational Learning Support Programme. The programme supports the delivery of high–quality vocational learning, including vocational GCSEs, A levels and other work-related learning, with help for practitioners and learners at both 14–16 and 16–19.'

Continuing professional development (CPD)
Lifelong Learning UK – http://www.lifelonglearninguk.org/
Lifelong Learning UK is the Sector Skills Council responsible for the professional development of all those working in further education and in some other post-16 sectors. All the previous information on the FENTO (Further Education National Training Organisation) has now been transferred to the Lifelong Learning UK site.

Unitary awarding bodies
The following sites provide all the information you need to know about becoming an examiner or moderator:
Edexcel – http://www.edexcel.org.uk/home/
OCR – http://www.ocr.org.uk/
AQA – http://www.aqa.org.uk/

Research networks
Research Network – http://www.lsneducation.org.uk/
British Educational Research Association – http://www.bera.ac.uk/
Society for Research into Higher Education – http://www.srhe.ac.uk/

Name Index

Ainley, Patrick   2
Allan, J. 42–3

Cackowski, Z.   45
Chandhari, V. S.   43
Cropley, A.J.   29
Curtis, P.   7
Curzon, L.B.   44

Davies, T.   24
Dearing, Sir Ron   17

Flanders, N.A.   59

Gartside, P.   42–3
Golden, S.   5

Higham   6
Hodgson, Ann   2, 10

Jones, T.P.   45

Kingston, P.   1

Labelle, B.   45

McFarlane, A.E.   24
Miliband, David   5
Milton, David   30
Morris, Estelle   2

Ogunleye, James   22, 24, 27, 38,
   40, 49–50, 53, 57, 64, 71

Parnell, Dave   38
Pratt, H.   26

Robinson, Ken   34

Sale, D.   29
Sproson, B.   22
Spours, Ken   2, 10
Stevenson, R.B.   47

Tomlinson, Sir Mike   6

qualification
  academic   18–19
  vocational   16–21
  national qualification
    framework   16
Qualifications and Curriculum
  Authority   11, 15–17

reform
  highlights   3
  policies   1–2
  reasons   2
report
  Dearing   17
  NACCCE (National Advisory
    Committee on Creative and
    Cultural Education)   **34**
  Tomlinson   1, 6, **7, 9,** 10
    see also 14–19 Working
    group

scheme of work   26
Scottish Qualifications
  Authority   15, 17
self-confidence
  student   44, 58, 63, 79, 82
student
  classroom behaviours   58
  creative thinking skills   77
  praise   54–5, 82
  self-confidence   44, 58, 63, 79,
    82
  sustain interest   52–3, 81
subjects
  core national curriculum   11,
    13

vocational   12, 15, 21
  options   13

teacher
  classroom behaviours
    58–9
  confidence   24
  emphasis on content   61
  enthusiasm   25
  knowledge   24
  professionalism   26
  question ratio   60
  reference to real-life   62
  response ratio   61
  talk   60
teaching
  aids   31
  materials   30–1
  styles   45, 66, 77, 79
  techniques   35
  techniques, for *14–16* year
    olds   36, 76
  techniques, for *16–19* year
    olds   42, 78
  techniques, for *14–19* year olds
    mixed group   48, 80

vary
  lesson paces
  teaching styles   39, 45, 66, 77,
    79
vocational
  elements   11
  options   13
widening
  participation   2–3

Subject Index

A number in *italics* indicates a figure; **bold** indicates a more significant section within a sequence of pages.

academic
 curriculum   15, 21
 qualifications   **17–20**
achievement
 rates at *16*   2
action research   70, 85
aids
 teaching   31
awarding bodies   18
 AQA   18, 67
 Edexcel   18, 67
 OCR   18, 67

behaviour   58, 63
 behavioural problem   63
 managing behaviours   40, 63, 78

case for reform   1
class
 mixed-age   56
classroom
 behaviours   58
challenge students   77
collaboration   14
collaborative work   4
continuing professional
  development   63, 66, **83–4**
continuing professional
  development plan   66, **83–5**

core
 elements   11
 entitlement   11
creative
 abilities   34–5
 challenge   33, 41, 76
 lesson   36, 76
 lesson plan   22, 26–7, 28, 32
 interaction   58
 teaching techniques   36
 teacher   33, 76
 thinking   37–8, 45, 77
creativity   22, 29, **33–6**, 63, 65, 71, 72, 83, 85
creativity definition   34
creativity in learning and
  teaching   63
creativity, nourishing agents
  72–3, 85–6
creativity, personal development
  71–2, 85
curriculum
 academic
 Curriculum *2000*   10, 19
 key stage   4, 11
 national curriculum   4, 11, **13**, 34
 national curriculum subjects
  11, 13
 vocational   12, 15, 21

diplomas 6, 9, 12, 21
  framework 8, 12
drop out rates 2

education
  formal 2
  14–19 phase 1–2, 6, 10
  16–19 phase 14
examination
  boards 15, 67, 73
  marking process 68
  see also awarding bodies
external
  examiner 84
  moderator 69, 84
  verifier 69, 84–5

government
  Conservative 3
  Labour 1, 3
group
  cohesiveness 81
  mixed age 48
  work 58
  14–19 Working group 1, 6–7, 10
    see also Tomlinson
handout
  informational 30

knowledge
  of *14–19* provision 71

learning
  aids 82
approach 58
  enterprise 4
  materials 30–1
  preference 58
  work-related 4
lesson
  hook points 26
  introductions 36, 76

paces 36–7, 76
plan 22, 24, 26–7, 29, 37, 75
planning 75
preparation 75
starters 36, 76, 80

moderation 69

pathfinders 1, **5–6**
personal
  development in creativity 71–2, 85
  and professional development 66, 71, 73
planning
  lesson 23–6, 29, 48, 56, 78
presentation
  lesson 24–6, 29, 48, 56, 75
problem
  solving 45, 80
  behavioural 63
professional development 65
  forms of professional development 67
programme
  increased flexibility 1, 4, **5**, 10, 12
provision
  14–16 provision 11
  16–19 provision 14
  14–19 provision 1
  Key stage *4* provision 14

question 43, 63
  open-ended 43, 77, 78
  closed 43, 79
  ratio 60
  students' questions 57
questioning 57, 78
  skills 37–8, 43
  techniques 78